OUTTAKES
DAN PATRICK

EDITED BY JOHN HASSAN

ESPN
BOOKS

HYPERION
NEW YORK

This book is for my mother Patti, my father Jack and my brothers and sisters: Mike, Bill, Dave, Ann and Molly. They made every dinner conversation our version of "Outtakes."

ACKNOWLEDGMENTS

As is clear by now, these interviews were originally done for *ESPN The Magazine*. I'd like to thank everybody at the magazine for their help, especially Pamela Miller, John Papanek, John Skipper, Jessie Paolucci, Jeanine Melnick, Tricia Reed, Peter Yates and John Broder ("Kruk" to his friends). A special nod goes to John Hassan; he's really just a highly paid messenger boy but he's *my* highly paid messenger boy. He has proven to be invaluable. At Hyperion, I want to thank Bob Miller, Gretchen Young and Jennifer Morgan.

During my time working on *SportsCenter*, I have gotten many uncredited assists from Pete McConville, Todd Snyder, Jeff Bennett and the dean of sports statistics and information, Howie Schwab.

At ESPN, where synergy is more than a fancy word to use at board meetings, there are a lot of people who make it possible for me to work these 27-hour days for *SportsCenter*, the *Magazine*, SportsCentury and ESPN Radio. I'd like to thank John Walsh, Steve Anderson, Norby Williamson, Mark Shapiro, Len Weiner and Eric Schoenfeld. I'd also like to thank my agent Steve Lefkowitz, who strikes all these deals for me. He gets ten percent but I know he gives me eleven.

My heartiest and heartfelt thanks to the aforementioned friends and colleagues. But the real credit, and none of the blame, for what I do goes to my wife, Sue. From our first date, on which I brought exactly as much money as we spent on those four beers, through twelve years of marriage and four beautiful children, she has always been there for me. Sue, I owe my success to you.

INTRODUCTION

My life has always been centered around tennis. For over a decade, week to week I play tournaments, circling the globe with one focus: winning on the court. Luckily, I have been able to achieve this goal (most of the time), and, quite honestly, when I look back on my accomplishments I simply can't believe it. All the sweat, the tears, the vomiting... And sure, I've won Wimbledon six times (whatever) and I have been ranked number one in the world six years in a row (so what?).

Interviewing is not my favorite part

But do you want to know what really stands out for me? The most poignant part of my career? My "Outtakes" interview with Dan Patrick in *ESPN The Magazine.*

Why?

Because when I'm on Center Court at Wimbledon, fighting for my life, to whom do I look for inspiration? I'll give you a hint. He's on center stage himself. He does Coors commercials (Who's his agent?). Yes, I think about what Dan would do if he were in this situation—when he's sitting there at the console, lights beaming on the top of his head, the clock ticking and the commercial is ending. That's the kind

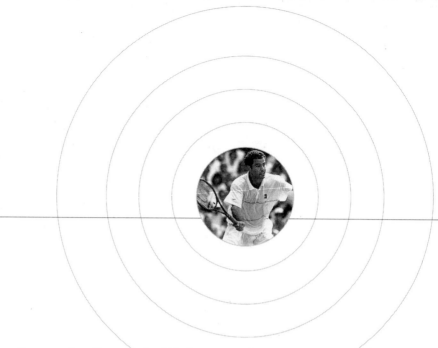

of pressure I could never take. He's da man. You know. When he's *en fuego*.

Now, I'm not going to lie. Interviewing is not my favorite part of being a professional athlete. Week after week, year after year, it's the same questions and the same stories. But I actually look forward to talking to Dan because he cuts below the surface. He's interested in what's beyond the outer layer. And he's funny. An interviewer can either bring out the real person or they can be lazy

of being a professional athlete.

and regurgitate (no pun intended) the same old boring (again, no pun) stuff that's out there. The result can't help but be a bit dull. I do between 80 and 100 interviews a year, and believe me, if every interviewer had the talent and personality that Dan has, I'd be the most interesting man on the planet!

So enjoy these "Outtakes." You'll see what I mean.

Pete Sampras

P.S. Dan, please make the check out to Pistol Pete, Inc. Thanks.

OUTTAKES

CONTENTS

26	**32**	**38**	**44**
Dale Earnhardt	Steve Young	Tim Duncan	Eric Lindros
74	**80**	**86**	**92**
Jeff Gordon	Doug Flutie	Shannon Sharpe	John Randle
122	**128**	**134**	**140**
Tony Gwynn	Tom Glavine	Julie Foudy	Barry Sanders

DAN PATRICK   BRETT FAVRE

When we lose in Minnesota,

$\mathbf{T}$ he first time I met the pride of Kiln, MS, we were playing in a golf tournament. After a few holes, I told him I knew why his jersey number was four. Get it? Anyway, Brett was good-natured about the ribbing. He just laughed and said, "I'll never look at my number the same way. F-o-r-e." No "NFL MVP" ego that I could see.

When I was trying to track Brett down for this interview, I had to look all over for him. I could have sworn he was supposed to call me. As it turns out, he was doing what he often does in the off-season; having some shrimp at his golf club, while he waited for *me* to call *him*.

Before the interview, his "people" wanted me to fax the questions in advance. Normally, I don't go for that kind of thing. I usually do some research in advance, but I mostly try to have an off-the-cuff interview that reflects the athlete's personality rather than pursue a strict line of inquiry. There aren't many topics that I have lined up in advance. So I faxed over a list of questions that I might ask Brett Favre. Or Cameron Diaz. Or Walter Cronkite. Still, I was nervous. When somebody asks for an advance peek, you usually get a guarded, uninformative interview. And this was the first "Outtakes" for the premiere issue of *ESPN The Magazine*.

So I asked Brett if he got the questions I sent over. He seemed puzzled and just said, "No. Ask whatever you want." And I did.

DP: First of all, how would you rate **the moustache** you're wearing on the cover of your autobiography?

BF: Oh man...I've gotten more grief about my moustache, my sideburns...

DP: I thought you were doing one of those milk ads.

BF: (Laughs.) It does look a lot like that...it's a darn shame.

DP: **You look like a porno star.**

BF: Dirk Diggler.

I cry all the way home.

DP: If we were playing a pick-up game in **Kiln, Miss.** in somebody's backyard or you were playing a game against the Bears at Lambeau, would your attitude on winning be any different?

BF: No. I enjoy playing whether it's golf or football, whether it's the Super Bowl or preseason. **I want to play well no matter what. The stakes for me are the same.**

DP: If you don't win another Super Bowl, can you still lay claim to being one of the greatest quarterbacks of all time? Or is the bottom line, for you, measured in championships and nothing else?

BF: I think a lot of it has to do with how many championships you win. And a lot of *that* has to do with who you play with. A lot of great quarterbacks have never won a Super Bowl, and may never win a Super Bowl, but are still great quarterbacks. I look at it two ways. I think winning championships is important but the most important thing is: How good are you? **Can you play? That's the bottom line.** I think I've proven it so far.

DP: Did you ever doubt your abilities?

BF: I do every day. I think I do it on purpose. That's what motivates me. Waking up saying, "I don't know if I can do it." And working hard to tell my mind over and over again that I can't do it and working and working and then doing it and going, "See!" It's kind of got me into a pattern, a work ethic, that I never even dreamed I would have.

DP: Do you understand what a defensive player thinks and what he feels and how he acts?

BF: I think so. I think that's what's helped me. I really do. **I think my mentality toward the game has enabled me to be a good player. By playing balls out.** But quarterbacks are supposed to be different. I was worried about that.

DP: You hate being viewed that way, don't you?

BF: Yeah. **I want to go out and I want to kick ass.** You tell me what you want me to do and I'll do it. That's the way I play the game. And I always thought that was the way everyone played the game but... apparently not.

DP: Would you cheat to win?

BF: **In golf, yeah.** (Both laugh.) Just the other day I moved my ball in the rough a little bit. But football, no. It's too important for me. Sure, I could go out and play golf and lose twenty bucks and move my ball in the rough and not worry about it. But in football, I could never do that.

DP: If the public was allowed in the Packers huddle, what would we be surprised about with you?

BF: Probably my approach. **The way I'll jokingly approach the game.** If you saw me in the huddle during a TV time-out and a song is playing and all of a sudden I'll start singing in the huddle or cracking a joke or doing whatever.

DP: You haven't passed gas in the huddle, have you?

BF: Oh, I tell you what, there was one game this year and I had gas so bad. I had beans the night before and you could smell it at the line. **It was awful.** It may have helped us that game. (Much raucous laughter.)

DP: How do you keep receivers happy? Because they're always open when they come back to the huddle, aren't they?

BF: I think our guys know ahead of time that I don't care who's catching the passes. I'm throwing to the open guy or whatever my read is. I've lost a lot of receivers throughout the course of a season and we just go on like nothing ever happened. And I don't bitch either. Never bitched at a receiver, never bitched at our running backs, never bitched at our linemen. If I get sacked, I just get up. One of our linemen will say, "Brett, I'm sorry." I say, "Don't worry about it, man." You know, I throw bad passes. **I don't want you mad at me when I throw a bad pass.**

DP: Are there days when you've gone out on Lambeau Field and just wanted to cry it was so cold?

BF: Yes. There's probably been three games, the Raiders my first year, the Rams my second year, and Carolina in 1997 was just brutal. **Really cold. No fun. You couldn't wait to get it over.**

DP: Except for winning the Super Bowl, what was the greatest moment you ever had in football no matter what age you were?

BF: One of the most memorable moments was my last game in high school. My dad was my coach. I didn't know what the future was going to hold for me and at that particular time I didn't care. It was like, "I can't believe this is over." You can't wait to graduate and all of a sudden it's there. My dad had coached me forever, too. He coached baseball when I was a little kid. I remember sitting in the locker room just crying before the game even started. Win or lose, I didn't really care. That was a tough moment but it is one that when I'm seventy years old I'll remember.

DP: Is that the last time you cried in regard to football?

BF: **No. I'm a tough loser. I really hate to lose.**
I relate things to golf because I do it every day when I'm not playing football. When I lose, the drive home is not fun. Now imagine football. When we lose to Minnesota in Minnesota, I cry all the way home. I can't even talk to anyone. I work too hard to lose a ball game, that's the way I look at it. Some guys don't approach it that way. It's like, well, I got paid, hell. But I think it's a slap in my face and my family's face to lose. **When we lose, I cry.**

DP: Are people uncomfortable being around you because they don't know what they can or what they can't talk about with you?

BF: Certain people. Although I think I've surrounded myself with people who don't care who I am and that's important to me. To be able to go out and do something and guys can just go, "Hey, you piece of shit!" I'll laugh at that. I relish that. Instead of pulling a drive 300 yards into the woods and somebody going, "That was a great shot!" That gets old. You know, **after a while, you just want to be one of the guys.**

DP: If you didn't play anymore, what would you do?

BF: Well, my wife would kill me, but I'd probably play golf every day. Hunt, golf and fish...that's probably it.

DP: If owners really love football, they would what...?

BF: Shorten preseason probably. They need to make money like we do. I understand that. But midway through the season I think, "God, we've still got another half to go?"

DP: If it's not about the money, what is it about?

BF: With me, it's the competition. But I still can't believe we make the money we make to play this game. I love to play but to think that we make all this money is amazing.

DP: I think what struck me was the first time I realized I made more money than my father...

BF: Yeah, isn't that crazy? **My Dad, in thirty years of coaching and teaching, never made, altogether, what I make in two weeks.** That's scary.

DP: If you could change any rule in pro football...

BF: I've probably got a million of them, but...

DP: Nothing really jumps out? What about "in the grasp"?

BF: Well, it never really bothered me because I'm always moving around and getting out of stuff. There's never been a play where I knew I was going to get out of it but they blew the whistle.

DP: Instant replay—yes or no?

BF: Don't care either way. I think it works out either way. It evens out.

DP: All right, free association. Sherm Lewis.

BF: Super guy, excellent coach.

DP: Pain.

BF: Part of the game.

DP: Anger.

BF: Once again, part of the game.

DP: John Elway...don't say part of the game!

BF: (Laughs.) Well, he's part of the game.
<u>John Elway,</u> good friend and just a great quarterback.
I can't say enough about him.

DP: Dallas Cowboys.

BF: My favorite team growing up.

DP: (Laughs.) But did you grow to hate them?

BF: No, I never hated them. I really didn't. **They were a pain in
my ass, but it was no one's fault but ours.** We couldn't
beat 'em 'cause we weren't worth a shit.

DP: Isn't that difficult, though? Here's a team that you would do anything
to play for and now you have to try to beat 'em and you can't beat 'em.

BF: Everyone hated them. My wife hated them. Our team hated them. But
I look at things pretty realistically. They're kicking our ass but there's
no reason for me to hate them.

DP: Binge food.

BF: It's funny you said that... **shrimp.**
Anything to do with shrimp...I gotta
eat it. Fried, baked...I mean, I sound like
Bubba Gump.

DP: I know you do...you sound like Forrest Gump.

BF: Anything with shrimp, I gotta eat it.
And I don't get it in Green Bay, obviously.
When I come home, I eat fried shrimp at
the club every day.

DP: If you could be another player ...

BF: I would like to be Reggie White.
<u>I don't understand how he could take</u>
a guy fifty pounds heavier than him
and throw him that way. That to me
is unbelievable. I've seen him do
some things that I didn't think were
physically possible.

I'd like to see what they

reg Maddux and I spoke during the 1998 season the day after he lost a game that would have been his 200th career win. He had to be pulled away from a card game in the Braves clubhouse but he got on the phone with me because he'd said he would. We started off with some small talk about the game but he wasn't particularly upset. He knew he'd be pitching in five days and would just try again. I don't think he would have been any different if he had gotten that milestone victory. He still would have been playing cards, waiting for his next start.

The first time I did a Sunday conversation with Maddux for ESPN, I have to admit that I did not recognize him at first. He had his glasses on and he walked into the room with little of the flair and strut that so many professional athletes display. I quickly realized, however, that my guest had arrived—and that the unassuming quality he brings to the mound is with him in real life too.

Don't make the mistake, though, of thinking that Maddux is some pushover. He won't be rattled. To show how old I am, I'll use a metaphor from my childhood: Even if the world around him is going 45 or even 78 rpms, Greg Maddux stays right at 33 $\frac{1}{3}$.

GM: Hey, Dan. How're you doing?

DP: Good. You pretty excited about this?

GM: About...?

DP: ...Doing this interview?

GM: Oh, I'm just fired up.

DP: (Laughs.) I told Glen (the PR guy) that I openly rooted for the Braves last night. I thought that I wanted you to be in a good mood for this. But he said, "Well, you know what, you can't tell the difference if he just won or if he just lost."

are *not* hitting.

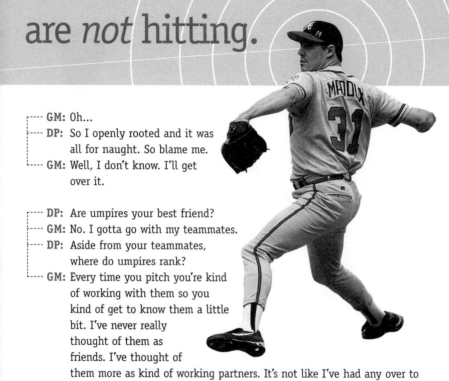

GM: Oh...

DP: So I openly rooted and it was all for naught. So blame me.

GM: Well, I don't know. I'll get over it.

DP: Are umpires your best friend?

GM: No. I gotta go with my teammates.

DP: Aside from your teammates, where do umpires rank?

GM: Every time you pitch you're kind of working with them so you kind of get to know them a little bit. I've never really thought of them as friends. I've thought of them more as kind of working partners. It's not like I've had any over to my house for dinner. I think it's only right that you keep your distance.

DP: Is *Silence of the Lambs* still your favorite movie?

GM: (Pause.) Yeah. It probably still is.

DP: **If Hannibal Lecter was in baseball, who would Hannibal be?**

GM: Wow. Wow. (Pause.) I don't know.

DP: Is it safe to assume that he would be an owner?

GM: Ummmm, maybe not. Who knows? Let me see. Who would be Hannibal Lecter? (Long pause.) God, this is a tough one. Probably **Rudy Seanez.**

DP: Really. Why?

GM: I don't know. I get that feeling about him, man. You never know.

DP: (Laughter.) Does Rudy know you think this about him?

GM: He has no idea.

DP: What's with the Mickey Mouse watch that your wife gave you?

GM: Mickey's pretty cool. (Laughs.)

DP: (Laughs.) That's it?

GM: Well, OK, I'm not going to get a nice watch. I'll end up losing it. Leaving it at one of the hotels.

DP: Three hitters you think are smarter than you.

GM: Only three? There's probably three on every team.

DP: Oh, come on.

GM: You never really know what the guy's thinking or what he's looking for.

DP: Just guys that you say, "He's figured me out."

GM: Mark Grace. Tony Gwynn. Barry Bonds.

DP: So you are back to the drawing board for those guys?

GM: Yeah, those and about 300 or 400 other guys. (Laughter.)

DP: What is the nicest thing a hitter ever said to you?

GM: Andre Dawson said,

"I'll play behind him any time."

DP: You are listed at 6'0", 175. Are we lying about that?

GM: Maybe 180-185, somewhere in there.

DP: So you are actually bigger than that?

GM: Fatter.

DP: Do you consciously want batters to hit balls back to you?

GM: No. **I'm the last guy I want them to hit it to.**

DP: But you're a great fielder.

GM: Yeah, but you have to understand that it's a lot easier for the guy standing a hundred feet away to field it than it is for me standing about fifty feet away.

DP: Have you ever thought about wearing your glasses on the mound?

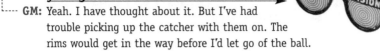

GM: Yeah. I have thought about it. But I've had trouble picking up the catcher with them on. The rims would get in the way before I'd let go of the ball.

DP: So this "Professor" nickname, have you fully embraced that or do you like "Mad Dog" better?

GM: I kind of like **"Doggie"** better, to be honest with you.

DP: **Because "Professor" doesn't sound too macho, does it?**

GM: Well, nobody calls me "Professor" but the media. (Much laughter.)

DP: OK. So blame it on the media?

GM: Well, I mean, you know, no one else calls me that.

DP: OK. You see I get all my information from Jeff Blauser.

GM: Well, you gotta remember the source.

DP: Can anyone calm Leo Mazzone down during a game?

GM: No. (Laughs.)

DP: Does he make you nervous when you look over and see him?

GM: You get used to it. **It's like you get nervous if he's not rocking.** It's to the point that if he's not nervous, you say, "What's wrong? Why are you so calm?"

DP: First and second, nobody out and Griffey, Gonzalez, Thome and Rodriguez all coming up. **1998 All Star game.** What are you thinking?

GM: Only give up one or two. (Laughs.) You're thinking right there, stay out of the big inning. You know? If you're down 2-0 at Coors Field, it's no big deal. You just don't want to go down 3,4,5. Basically, you just try to get the next three guys out. **Hey, if you give one or two, suck on it. No big deal.**

DP: Do pitchers ever give up a home run on a good pitch?

GM: Rarely. Very rarely.

DP: So if Ken Caminiti hits a homer off you, did he hit a good pitch or a bad pitch?

GM: The one last night was a bad pitch.

DP: Bad pitch in your mind?

GM: In my mind, yeah. Good pitch for him, bad pitch for me.

DP: So you have thrown a good pitch before and somebody's homered?

GM: I have. Yeah. What I felt was a good pitch. The pitch I tried to throw.

DP: Describe the sound of a home run.

GM: # Maybe like two cars crashing right in front of you.

DP: And you never get that sound out of your head?

GM: There's a certain echo that goes on.

DP: Has *SportsCenter* made you a better pitcher?

GM: Yeah, it hasn't hurt, that's for sure. I think the more you see, the more you have a chance to learn. You get to see a lot of pitches on *SportsCenter*. I wish they'd show more strikeouts, I know that. I'd like to maybe see what they're *not* hitting as opposed to what they are hitting. (Laughs.)

DP: Free association. **Bud Selig.**

GM: Owner.

DP: **Mark McGwire.**

GM: Power hitter.

DP: **Jack Nicklaus.**

GM: Good golfer.

DP: **Nintendo.**

GM: Makes your eyes go bad. (Laughs.)

DP: **Juggs gun.**

GM: Overrated.

DP: I was going to say "Jeff Blauser" but I was afraid you would say "overrated" again.

GM: **No lips, big chin.**

DP: When is the last time you asked for a batting tip?

GM: Two days ago.

DP: Who did you ask and what about?

GM: Clarence Jones. I asked him, "CJ, why am I getting jammed?"

DP: What did CJ say?

GM: He said two reasons. **You suck and you're jumping too much. I said OK.**

DP: Do you wish you were a position player at times?

GM: Never.

DP: Why?

GM: I enjoy the four off-days. I have a very easy time sitting still. I enjoy sitting on the bench watching the games.

DP: As a fan, would you rather watch a great pitching performance or a great hitting performance?

GM: Pitching, any day of the week.

DP: But you can see that when you pitch.

GM: No.

DP: Yeah, you can. But you wouldn't admire it if McGwire hit three homers or **Griffey** had four doubles.

GM: No. I'd be more impressed by someone striking those guys out three or four times a night than seeing them hit two or three out.

DP: Do you derive any greater pleasure by striking out a big name than you would a ground ball to shortstop?

GM: Not necessarily.

DP: Mano a mano, you against McGwire, you don't derive any greater satisfaction. I bet he would.

GM: The thing is too that **when you strike someone out, you give them something to remember about you.**

DP: You're kind of like that dog that just bites at the pant leg.

GM: (Laughs.)

DP: You're there, you just annoy but you don't want to take a big bite so they come back and want to hit you with the newspaper.

GM: Just try to piss them off a little.

DP: Now I know why they call you Doggie. It's a small, fat dog. But it's biting your pant leg. I understand that now! I can mention this on *SportsCenter!*

DP: You ever have nightmares where you've lost it? What kind of thought process happens where you think, "I could turn into Joe Cowley, Steve Blass or Mark Wohlers"?

GM: You just blow it off when it crosses your mind.

DP: But how does it enter your mind?

GM: Who knows? **You sit around by yourself long enough and you're going to start thinking of some pretty stupid things.**

I got the whip. I got the top hat. You

I met Dennis Rodman early in his career, when he was with the Pistons. We were in a bar and he was quietly playing "Pop-a-Shot" and keeping to himself. You couldn't tell who he was or what he did for a living. Quiet, unassuming. And then the transformation took place: tattoos, piercings, cross-dressing. He's probably the same guy, but now there are all these layers to get past.

Today, when you are with Dennis, you get the sense that he is not all there, that he is perpetually distracted. In this interview, he calls me Chris. He has also called me Craig and Bob. He never knows my name. And you never know what he's going to do. There is more stuff from this interview that can't be used than from any other one I've done. Just too weird. Too scary.

This bit of intercourse took place at Eric Clapton's apartment on South Beach in Miami during 1999 Super Bowl week. Dennis was getting ready to go out. He had a makeup artist with him. The NBA lockout was still on, but Dennis was talking about where he wanted to play. Other things came up too. With Dennis, they always do.

DP: What went wrong with the Bulls? How did it all fall apart?

DR: I don't think it fell apart. I think that everybody had an indifference on what went on over those last few years, Michael coming back, Scottie having contract problems, Phil having a little resentment towards a lot of things with the organization. But there was no hatred. It was just the fact that **the business part got in the way of everything else.**

DP: What is your motivation to play?

DR: Well, there isn't any motivation to play. I think it's just more like the fact that people want to see me play, because you know, besides me

name it, I got it, baby.

just playing, I'm an entertainer. And you really don't get that in players today, okay? You won't get the Dennis Rodmans out there anymore. You don't get all the **Cirque du Soleil,** as you want to call it.

DP: So you want to continue, but it's your own circus.

DR: It's my own show. It's my own show. **I got the whip.** I got the top hat. I got the glasses. I got everything. I got the color. You name it—I got it, baby.

DP: Where do you want to play?

DR: It doesn't really matter where I play. I think it's just the fact that I can go out there and be competitive.

DP: But you want to win.

DR: Of course.

DP: I think one of the things that you have been slighted on is you've been a winner pretty much wherever you have gone.

DR: Everywhere I've been, even with **San Antonio.** We came this close to being in the finals in the Western Conference. And people haven't given me the credit. They say, you were a distraction down there. I was a distraction down there, but for some reason they trade me to the Bulls and all of a sudden three years later what happened? He may cause a lot of bumps in the road, but the bumps seem to smooth themselves out.

DP: But you want to win another title.

DR: If I do anything, it has to be with a team that can win.

DP: Miami has a chance to win.

DR: Miami has all the elements. Good elements. And bad elements. And this South Beach is bad. Because you know me. **I like to stray every once in a while.** Miami has a great chance of winning. I'm not a bench player. So if I come here, I'm going to have to come out there balls to the walls. I've got to go out there and start. Because I'm too old to be coming off the bench and try to teach players how to play.

DP: Can you coexist with Riley and Mourning?

DR: Why would I worry about any individual? Riley is Riley. Mourning is Mourning. When you're working with them you get along because you are all trying to get to here, trying to get to that goal, basically. **I can give a damn if Pat Riley likes me,** Alonzo Mourning likes me, anybody on that team likes me. But when we get on that floor that's when we all get together and try to win a championship.

DP: Where are you leaning towards?

DR: Right now I'm not leaning towards anything. I just want to kinda make the circuit right now. Get all of the parties out of the way. Get all the distractions out of the way. I need to go somewhere where there's not too much distraction.

DP: Then you can't go to Miami, with South Beach.

DR: If I go to Orlando it's the same thing. South Beach is what, a half-hour trip? I can't do that. I'd rather be down there because there's less. I have no friends. I have nobody down there to go, "Dennis, let's go do this." I would be able to focus and try to win.

DP: So Orlando would be a better option.

DR: I think it would be a better option for me. **I can't go to Toronto. That sucks.** I can't go to Vancouver. I can't stand that. I can't go anywhere where I have to teach. If the price was right with New York, great. Maybe I would think about it. But I want to go somewhere that is warm. Where my body can be as one when I wake up in the morning.

DP: Do you worry about not being able to entertain once you're through with the NBA, having that stage every single night?

DR: I never worry about that because **I create my own destiny.** You have to understand something, Chris. I'm very international. So I'm not worried about people saying, "OK, great, he used to be this, but now he's this. So we have to forget about him." **I will keep myself in front of that damn lens right there as long as I live.** You don't have to worry about that. If it's basketball or wrestling, or movies or pornos. What do you want? (Laughter.)

DP: You're right. You're right. Geez, how could I forget pornos? How did that slip my mind? You're right, I forgot all about that. Children's books. You're going to do it all, I think.

DR: Absolutely.

DP: A ride at Disney World. We could call it The Worm.

DP: Your relationship with **Jordan.** Did it improve? Did it stay the same? Did you coexist?

DR: I think me and Michael had a fine line between each other. I think Michael really respected the fact that I came to play. He knew that I was going to go out there to bust my ass for the team. That's what he did. People put this persona on Michael. "You're God, so if you do anything wrong, **we're still going to kiss your ass."** OK. I don't blame him. I love Michael to death. He is a great guy. If he wanted to come back, I'd come back and play with him again.

DP: With **Latrell Sprewell** coming to New York, a lot was said about giving him **a second chance.** Have you ever gotten to a point where you would take matters into your own hands and go after a coach?

DR: We have a society where we always have to do something. We have to respond and say, "That's wrong." "That's not wrong." It should have never gotten to a public venue. When two players on the same team are fighting, that's no big deal. But, a coach and a player? It happens all the time. But it's never publicized. **Sprewell** was wrong. I think it was very damaging to his career and his life. But now he's got his life back.

Hopefully he can redeem himself. If he does, great. If he doesn't, then he will always be known as the guy that attacked his coach.

DP: He makes you look good though, doesn't he?

DR: I make money doing what I do. (Laughter.) I make money. What he did, that doesn't make money. He lost a lot of money. What I do is more like... I kick the cameraman. But you have to understand something, David Stern needs Dennis Rodman. The NBA needs Dennis Rodman to make money, just like Michael Jordan. I'm a commodity. Boom.

Here, use me. I'm your whore.
Great. Use me and now, pay me the money I deserve.

DP: When you look back at your career in Detroit and you see that Dennis Rodman — boyish looking, no tattoos, no hair coloring. Do you even know that Dennis Rodman?

DR: Yeah, I do. I see a kid that was

twenty-five years old. Didn't have no direction, no guidance, **no self-esteem,** no desire to be an individual or a man at that particular time.

DP: How's married life? How is Carmen?

DR: It's great. You know, everything's great.

DP: I didn't get you a wedding present. What do you get the guy who's got everything?

DR: Hmmm.

DP: Did you get any wedding gifts? Did Jordan or Pippen get you anything?

DR: Nobody gave me anything. It's amazing how all these athletes and famous people... People give these guys parties, celebrations, roasts and all that stuff. When it comes to me, I get none of that. I'm the Rodney Dangerfield of the NBA. They don't give a damn if I'm retiring or not, pretty much. Maybe the people, the public, the hard-working man, yes. But the NBA? Great, he's gone, goodbye. Enough of that. (Laughter.)

DP: How do you look in an Orlando uniform? Have you thought about that?

DR: How did I look in San Antonio? How'd I look in Chicago? I looked very good, didn't I?

DP: You looked good in Chicago. **You're not going to make good on your promise to strip in your last game on the floor, are you?**

DR: Why not? They already know that I'm going to do it. They can say that was just so bad. But people expect me to do it, basically. I guarantee when I do it **I'll get a standing ovation.** I'll walk off into the sunset pretty much.

DP: So that will be the final picture.

We'll see your ass going right up the tunnel walking away.

DR: Absolutely. Absolutely. You're going to get all of it. (Dennis acts like he's zooming a camera in tight and then he acts like he's licking something.) (Laughter.)

DP: You're a sad man. (Laughter.) Not that I need to come here to find this out. You're starting to scare me now. (Laughter everywhere.)

DP: We're done. I appreciate your time.

I am not a Cosby kid.

Ⓒharles Barkley watches more *SportsCenter* than most people do or should. He knows everybody and what they say and what they wear. He is always watching. And he is always listening.

Everybody knows that Charles can dish it out, but he can take it too. I have been around him many times. He likes to have a good time, and he doesn't have an air about him. You can give him grief. I can't see anybody trading barbs with Larry Bird or Michael Jordan, but Charles disarms you right away. He lets you know that you can speak your mind if you want. Actually, he is so approachable that it gets him in trouble.

There are many sides to Charles Barkley. You can ask him about black quarterbacks in the NFL or his favorite music, and you'll get a serious, con- sidered response that has some substance. Charles loves conversation, loves to talk. It's easy to dismiss him as a motor-mouth, but if you listen, you'll see that he has thought about what he says. There is a spontaneity in his actions that has gotten him into trouble, but I have always felt that his comments reveal a candor and degree of reflection that is unique, especially in this era of the sound bite. I'll miss him.

DP: Are you ready?

CB: I'm ready, my brother. I'm always ready. I'm living most people's dreams.

DP: Are you gonna say something stupid?

CB: No, baby. I'm here to intellectually stimulate America.

DP: **You're going to stimulate America?**
Oh, no. I should forewarn them then. Now, these questions are coming from all over the map. Are you ready? They won't be easy.

CB: Come on, Dan Patrick. Shut the hell up and get to it. By the way, is this going to be in **your little rip-off magazine?**

DP: Rip-off? We're reinventing. Anyway. Does a day go by that somebody

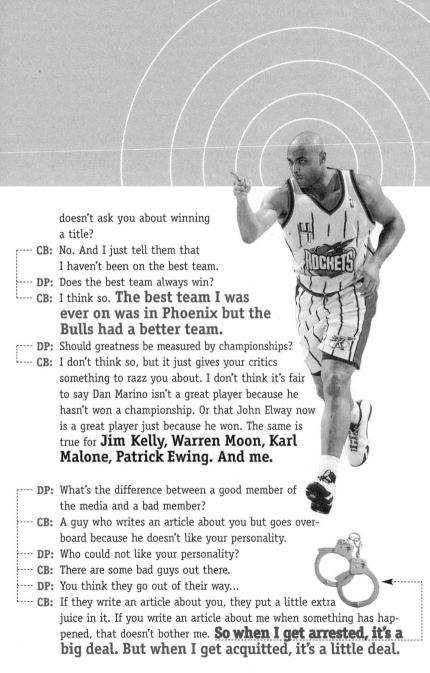

doesn't ask you about winning a title?

CB: No. And I just tell them that I haven't been on the best team.

DP: Does the best team always win?

CB: I think so. **The best team I was ever on was in Phoenix but the Bulls had a better team.**

DP: Should greatness be measured by championships?

CB: I don't think so, but it just gives your critics something to razz you about. I don't think it's fair to say Dan Marino isn't a great player because he hasn't won a championship. Or that John Elway now is a great player just because he won. The same is true for **Jim Kelly, Warren Moon, Karl Malone, Patrick Ewing. And me.**

DP: What's the difference between a good member of the media and a bad member?

CB: A guy who writes an article about you but goes overboard because he doesn't like your personality.

DP: Who could not like your personality?

CB: There are some bad guys out there.

DP: You think they go out of their way...

CB: If they write an article about you, they put a little extra juice in it. If you write an article about me when something has happened, that doesn't bother me. **So when I get arrested, it's a big deal. But when I get acquitted, it's a little deal.**

DP: But haven't you been involved in quite a few incidents?

CB: Only three. Orlando, Milwaukee and Cleveland. But they make it seem like it happens all the time. Complete strangers come up to me and say, "Don't punch me." The fans believe what they see on TV or what they read. That's my problem with the media.

DP: Has drinking been a problem when you go out?

CB: No. The only reason I stopped drinking is that I wanted to bring my team together. But I'm drinking. I drink two or three days a week and I like drinking. **There's nothing wrong with drinking.** I just did that to try and bring my team together. Just trying to do something to spark some community on this team.

DP: But you don't think you have a drinking problem?

CB: Not even close.

DP: Yeah, but automatically we think somebody has a problem when they say they have to stop drinking.

CB: I know for a fact that I don't have a drinking problem. I just wanted to spark the team, let them know how bad I wanted to win.

DP: Do you think you are one of the ten greatest players of all time?

CB: I don't think about stuff like that.

DP: You don't care how you're placed in history?

CB: I don't think people remember you when you retire. I've seen it too much. You know, we retired Moses Malone's jersey last week. I bet that was the first time somebody mentioned or thought about Moses since he retired. **I'm sitting here in Utah right now, looking up at Darrell Griffith's jersey. You think the Utah Jazz are concerned about him right now?**

DP: Clear something up for me. When you tried out for the Olympic team, you were clearly as good as anyone there but you didn't make the team.

CB: **I didn't want to make the team.**

DP: There was a rumor that you failed a drug test for pot.

CB: First of all, they never tested us for drugs. What happened was that I didn't want to make the Olympic team. I only tried out to move up in the draft. Once I had proven to everybody that I was one of the best, and I knew I would be one of the top five or six players taken, then we went home for a month. When we got back together, I didn't even try.

I told Steve Alford, my roommate, that I accomplished my goal and I didn't want to play basketball all summer.

DP: Give me three guys under 25 that you respect.

CB: Under 25? **Tim Duncan.** (Long pause.) Is **Grant Hill** under 25?

DP: No, but I can make him under 25 if you are running out of candidates.

CB: **Kevin Garnett.** And Kobe Bryant.

DP: You were running out of names there.

CB: It's hard to find guys that are good guys with a chance to be great, great players.

DP: Favorite teammate in your career.

CB: Rick Mahorn. It was fun. We worked well together. And he taught me a lot about the game.

DP: Anybody that you have met or played with that you just couldn't get along with?

CB: Armon Gilliam. We just never meshed. We looked at the game differently. He looked at individual statistics.

DP: Free association here. **Discipline.**

CB: The will to do whatever it takes to be successful.

DP: Flagrant fouls.

CB: Dangerous.

DP: "Seinfeld."

CB: Terrific.

DP: The next president.

CB: Colin Powell.

DP: Retirement.

CB: Exciting.

DP: Karl Malone.

CB: Great player.

DP: Dennis Rodman.

CB: Very good player.

DP: What CDs are in your stereo right now?

CB: That's a good question. Uncle Sam...Old Jackson 5. Michael Jackson is one of my favorites. A lot of Motown. I love Motown.

DP: Three biggest punks in the NBA.

CB: (Hems and haws.) Give me another word.

DP: Crybabies.

CB: Penny Hardaway. (Long pause.) **Put him down three times. He's that big of a baby.**

DP: Complains about everthing?

CB: Just not tough enough.

DP: Besides you, who is **the most misunderstood player in sports?**

CB: Deion Sanders. Deion is a great person.

DP: Do you think he adds to the misunderstanding?

CB: No. First of all, if you're black and have a strong personality, people get nervous. We still live in a racial society. A strong black personality is intimidating. People want you to be humble and stay in your place.

DP: You think the media wants black athletes to be...

CB: There's no question **they want black athletes to be humble little boys.** It's been proven over time.

DP: I've been around you a lot and I don't consider you a racist.

CB: I'm the least racist person in the world, but any time a black person talks about race, he's considered a racist.

DP: No. But what if I talk about it? Then I'm a racist.

CB: That's not true.

DP: You can get away with a lot more than I can.

CB: What do you mean? You have to be more specific.

DP: If I question someone's mental toughness or their ability to think...

CB: A black player.

DP: If I say that, someone will look at it as racist.

CB: But you can't let other people dictate what you think.

DP: It wouldn't change my opinion. I couldn't care less.

CB: We live in a racial society. That's wrong. You can't say anything about anybody.

DP: Do you think the league should embrace what you have done? As far as being a spokesperson for the league.

CB: Well, I have been a spokesperson for the league. And I have done some good things and bad things. But that just makes me human.

DP: But we embrace Michael Jordan or Grant Hill.

CB: America wants that. **America doesn't want any strong, opinionated black men.**

DP: Why do you say that? You don't scare me!

CB: I don't scare you but I scare white America.

DP: Why would you scare white America?

CB: Because I'm going to tell the truth. They don't want me to get on television and say that racism is still very prevalent and that there aren't enough black coaches. **They want me to shut up and make a lot of money. And make them a lot of money. That's true, Dan Patrick.**

DP: Don't you think it's too easy to say that you are not a role model?

CB: No. What happens is that when I speak, I always speak as a black man, not an athlete. Because of racism in America, black kids have low self-esteem, and the pride factor. They **only see three black people: athletes, entertainers and crooks.** I do a lot of talking to kids and 99% of them want to be athletes. They have no idea that they have a better chance to be a doctor or lawyer or engineer. They don't understand that. I want to tell them that they are not going to make it in professional sports. I want them to be doctors, lawyers, teachers, firemen and policemen. But every kid you talk to wants to be a basketball player. Because they are so focused on getting money. Another bad thing about America is that we tell kids that if you don't make a lot of money, you're not successful. That goes for white kids too.

DP: Have you put yourself in Grant Hill's situation, someone who appeals to black and white kids?

CB: He's black first.

DP: But he's like some character from "The Cosby Show."

CB: But most black people aren't the Huxtables. Most black people are like the Evans family from "Good Times." I represent the Evanses. I always tell myself, **"You are not a Cosby kid. You're one of the 'Good Times' kids."** I'm J.J.

DAN PATRICK   DALE EARNHARDT

I can still intimidate.

(L) et the record show that I had an appointment. I called when I was told to call. But Dale Earnhardt had to be pulled out of a Friday pre-race meeting to talk with me. And he stayed in pre-race meeting mode while we talked.

To say the least, he lived up to his reputation as "The Intimidator." He had me backpedaling on more than a few questions. I was glad I had done the research, because if I ventured into an area that he didn't have much to say about...well, he didn't say much about it. I had to move along pretty quickly.

Dale Earnhardt was an interview that I really wanted to do out of respect for his accomplishments and what he had done for his sport. But he came out of a strategy meeting to talk to this guy about Jeff Gordon and Johnny Cash and his first car. I couldn't get him to focus or relax. Interviews only work if you have a right time/right place scenario. I try to get something new in each interview, but I think Dale has been around long enough so that we already know as much about him as he wants us to know.

I felt like road kill when it was done. So, while I enjoyed the challenge and have great respect for Dale, don't make me do this again.

DP: Is speed an **aphrodisiac?**

DE: I think so. It has been with me. Throughout my career, when I wanted to drive a car I wanted to drive it fast. People that want to go fast may make good racers because speed is a thrill, an excitement.

DP: Settle the argument once and for all. **Are NASCAR drivers athletes?**

DE: (Long pause.) That's a question that's been asked for ninety-nine years. To endure four hours plus in a race car at the temperatures we endure, if you are not an athlete you will not win.

DP: Give me a sport that requires similar skills to that of a NASCAR driver.

DE: There isn't one.

DP: No?

DE: No. Maybe the concentration and focus of a tennis match. I think **tennis,** when it comes to the focus, could be the same. Because of the determination and focus and the hot temperatures and the endurance level you have to put up with in a NASCAR race. We don't have half-times or time outs or breaks. You go hard. Even on a caution or a pit stop, it's happening quickly. You're focusing. You're talking the whole time about what you can do to the car to make it better for the next run.
As far as endurance, I don't think there's a sport you can compare it with.

DP: Do you ever let your wife drive when you're in the car?

DE: Sure.

DP: Is she a better driver than you?

DE: She's not a better driver than me. She's a good driver. **But I'm more comfortable driving, no matter who's in the car with me.**

DP: Are you a backseat driver?

DE: Probably yes.

DP: Why is it Formula One drivers get the women?

DE: Hey, I've got a beautiful wife.

DP: But doesn't it seem like the models go out to see Formula One guys?

DE: I don't know. I've never been to a Formula One track.

DP: Do you think you still intimidate?

DE: Yes, I can still intimidate.

DP: How much of a role does luck play in NASCAR?

DE: On some days, it seems like 100%. But I think a good driver and a good team makes the luck.

DP: If you grew up in Annapolis, Maryland, instead of Kannapolis, North Carolina, would you still be a race car driver?

DE: If my dad was Ralph Earnhardt, yes.

DP: When did you become a **Braves fan?**

DE: I met Jody Davis about 15 years ago when he was playing for the Cubs. And then he went to the Braves for the last two or three years of his career. Then I met **Bobby Cox** and Ned Yost. And I got to be friends with them. Now Bobby, Ned and I talk frequently on the phone. We talk about what's going on with their teams. Now every chance I get to watch them on the tube, I get fired up about it.

DP: Is car racing a young man's sport?

DE: It's an innovative sport and it's a sport that has moved very fast in the last ten years. I think you have to stay on top of change. And I think that younger guys have adapted more to changes and the older guys are more set in their ways. It may take them longer to adjust. Still, **if you are winning races, you are adjusting pretty well.**

DP: Tell me why **Jeff Gordon is good** or bad for NASCAR?

DE: I don't think he's bad for NASCAR at all. He's young and aggressive and brings a fresh side to the sport. He brings younger people into the sport. He's an exciting driver and an exciting person to watch and try to figure out.

DP: When did NASCAR go from being sports to being **entertainment?**

DE: I think it's always been entertainment as much as it has been a sport.

I think all forms of racing, or football or whatever, have always been entertaining.

I enjoyed racing before I was a driver. And I still enjoy racing even if I'm not in the race, and I'm talking about watching a truck race or a Busch race. I'm a Formula One fan when it comes to watching them on TV.

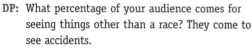

DP: What percentage of your audience comes for seeing things other than a race? They come to see accidents.

DE: There's always that factor. But I don't think it's as many as come to see close and competitive racing. I think they are more excited about the thrill of seeing someone racing side by side and one get beat and one win.

I don't think seeing an accident is the main focus.

DP: Do you worry that it's getting too big too soon?

DE: Well, I don't know if it's too big too soon rather than just too big sometimes.

DP: There are so many stops now.

DE: The schedule may be getting too tight. You can, I think, overdo it. If you only had a certain number of races, you might go more often because if the season was over you wouldn't want to say, "Well, I didn't get a chance to go." Now, there's one every weekend, so you'll say well, I'll give this one up. I'll go next weekend. Or next month for that matter.

DP: What question tips you off that someone doesn't know NASCAR?

DE: I can't really put my finger on anything that indicates someone doesn't understand the sport.

DP: Maybe you get a question that makes you say, "This person doesn't understand NASCAR."

DE: But you can't really hold that against somebody. What you do is try to educate them with answers.

DP: But you must get tired of answering those questions.

DE: But that goes back **to accepting your position of being not only a driver but also an ambassador for your sponsor or your sport.** You put yourself in that position to sign autographs or answer questions or do appearances.

DP: Will the <u>1998 Daytona winner's circle</u> be your fondest memory, even if you go on to other wins at Daytona?

DE: It is one of the greatest moments in my career. That and all the other championships, too. I think I've had as much fun or more fun winning championships as anything. It was pretty neat to keep winning championships. But I had never won the Daytona 500, so to finally win it in my 20th year and in the 50th year of NASCAR was pretty awesome.

DP: **To see all your competitors line up like that ... I don't care if you're not a NASCAR fan, people had to be moved by seeing that.**

DE: That meant as much to me as anything. That moved me so much. And all the faxes, phone messages and cards and notes that I have gotten. I have them in a big scrapbook that looks like I've been saving stuff in it for years and years on something. But it's just congratulations on the Daytona 500.

DP: The previous Daytona, weren't you in an accident and you said in the ambulance, "But there are still fenders on the car..."

DE: Tires. There are still tires on the car. I was getting in the ambulance and I looked back and I saw there were still front tires on this thing. So I jumped back out, went around and saw that all the tires were on it. I asked the guy in the car to see if it'll crank and he fired it off. So I told him, "Get out of the car! Get out of the car!" **And I jumped in and drove off.**

DP: Do people underestimate your determination, your drive to win?

DE: Maybe more in the last year of my career. People think, "Well, he's won seven championships. He's 47 years old. Maybe he's going to start to slow down." I think they are underestimating me when they do that. I'm still as determined, as aggressive and as positive as I can remember being.

Just don't get up against me when it's the wrong time because I'll put you where I want you.

DP: Why don't NASCAR drivers get tickets?

DE: Tickets?

DP: **Speeding tickets.**

DE: Oh, I thought you meant to the Bulls or something. I don't get any of those either.

DP: Michael just sends them to Jeff Gordon, he doesn't send them to you.

DE: I reckon. I just renewed my license back in April and in North Carolina if you don't have any tickets, you just get your picture made and take the eye test. That's all you have to do and I've done that for the last 15 years or so. I've not had a ticket.

DP: Free association. The color black.

DE: My black boots.

DP: **Johnny Cash.**

DE: I like.

DP: Richard Petty.

DE: The king.

DP: Fear.

DE: Budweiser.

DP: Fear, not beer!

DE: Budweiser.

DP: No, fear, f-e-a-r...

DE: Budweiser! No, I'll give you one for fear. (Pause) **I don't have any.**

DP: Dick Trickle.

DE: A great racer.

DP: Talladega.

DE: A great racetrack that needs to be raced on instead of restricted.

DP: Are you more nervous racing or watching your son race?

DE: I'm more nervous qualifying than either of those. But I'm probably more nervous watching him because of the confidence level. **If I knew he was as confident as I am capable, then I probably wouldn't be as nervous.** And it's not fear of him getting hurt but fear of him failing. Not being able to accomplish something going up against the competition.

DP: What does Jeff Gordon have that you don't?

DE: A lot of years left to race.

DAN PATRICK   **STEVE YOUNG**

Coaches make quarterbacks.

(**I**)n 1992, the Super Bowl was in Los Angeles and I was standing in the crowded lobby of the media hotel. Steve Young walked up to me with something on his mind. He admitted that he was tired of being criticized. He said, "I wish people would drop it. I can't be Joe Montana." He wasn't complaining or expressing any animosity towards Montana. He was just frustrated. As a member of the media, I appreciated the honesty and trust that he showed me. We talked a bit, and I told him to forget about the comparisons and to just be himself.

Six years later, Young gave me probably the best interview I have ever done. While I guess I had something to do with it, the results were mainly because Steve Young understands the give and take of reporting. He understood what I wanted to do and was willing to play. I realized pretty quickly that if I held up my end and asked some good questions, his responses would be just as good or better. He did his part too. His first comments indicate he had read my Brett Favre interview.

There was a spirit of competition too, in that I wanted to see if I could elicit some information from him that nobody else had gotten. And while Young is too smart to volunteer anything, he gave me anything I earned.

I did ask a Joe Montana question, but that's not a problem anymore.

DP: Good to talk to you.

SY: Thanks, but I don't know if I'm funny enough for this. We'll see. **I don't have any fart jokes.**

DP: You don't?

SY: No. I don't fart in the huddle.

DP: Have you ever tried to provide humor in the huddle?

SY: You have to. The TV timeouts are getting longer. It is a very weird time

Moms make running backs.

in a football game. The coaches freak because there's so much extra time to think about a play. They want to change it five times. What you do is not look over there. **They're waving their arms but you look somewhere else.** You just look in the stands for people you know.

DP: You've been hit so many times over your career. How do you take out your aggression?

SY: You take your beatings from the defensive linemen but you get a small degree of it back by making them run. One of my favorite things is to run a while just ahead of whoever it might be. Just to make them run all that time.

DP: Were you a good enough athlete early in your career to have played another position?

SY: When I was younger, I was pretty fast. I suspect that I could have played one of the two safety spots. But not running back. People think I could have been a running back because I can move around a bit. But there's no way.

DP: Why?

SY: Every other position is made but running backs are born.

DP: Are quarterbacks made?

SY: To a certain degree. A system helps, coaching and good fundamentals. At some level, if you are a great quarterback in the NFL, you were meant to be. It's too hard. But I still believe that you can coach a lot of quarterbacking. I don't see you coaching a running back that much. Coaches make quarterbacks. But moms make running backs.

DP: When did you realize that you were one of the great quarterbacks?

SY: I think Super Bowls do that. It helps *other* people get over the hump. **I won two MVPs before I won a Super Bowl. And people were still asking the same questions until I won the Super Bowl.** I felt like putting together three or four really top, solid years was what I had to do.

DP: What's your favorite USFL story?

SY: We played in the L.A. Coliseum, which is probably the greatest place to play football. So here we are in this fantastic stadium. But before the games, I would take thousands of tickets, literally, and pass them out to kids so that we would have fans. There were so few people that I actually had to whisper in the huddle. We'd move the huddle farther away so the defense couldn't hear. In the NFL, there's a whole shtick. There's between-play music, the natural noise of the crowd and the cheerleaders. In the USFL, there wasn't a sound.

DP: "Forever Young" sure sounds like an ambitious Web site.

SY: It's for charity, Dan! It's something for kids. Let's not overdo it. I'm not trying to claim anything. I'm just trying to raise some funds for kids. You're trying to ruin it.

DP: Great. Make me feel bad.

SY: **Typically cynical media!** I saw you coming from a long way away!

DP: When are you going to become an ineligible bachelor?

SY: I don't care how sappy it sounds. I'm waiting for the right girl.

DP: And you'll know. But you're engaged now, aren't you?

SY: I was.

DP: **So you're still eligible?**

SY: **Yes. Make sure that is prominently displayed, Dan. Great.**

DP: **What's the advantage to being a left-handed quarterback?**

SY: Generally, the right corner in this league is the weaker of the two. But that's my front side so I see it better. And right defensive ends are used to blindsiding quarterbacks. Defenses are usually set up to attack a right-handed quarterback from his backside. But that's my front side. Usually, the weaker pass rusher comes from your front side but that's my back side. When I was in college, the coach didn't want a lefty.

DP: Did Bobby Douglass of the Bears change all that?

SY: Bobby Douglass hurt us.

DP: He set left-handed quarterbacks back 20 years?

SY: With all that crazy running around.

DP: Oh, yeah. You never do that.

SY: It isn't crazy. Once everything breaks down, I move around. **People think Fran Tarkenton was a lefty. He's nuts. He must be a lefty.**

DP: Do you think it's a bias against left-handers that we can't view you guys as pure quarterbacks like Namath, Unitas and Marino? They're pure quarterbacks. You're a lefty.

SY: **A pure quarterback is a quarterback that can't move.** If you can move, you're a wild scrambler. I dropped back 4,000 times in college. As soon as I left the pocket, it was, "He's nuts. We cannot control him."

DP: When are you going to use this law degree?

SY: I use it subtly now. Referees are used to getting screamed at. I'm subtle. I use little walk-away statements. They notice it.

DP: If you are at a party, do you throw out legal terms to impress women?

SY: I'm not there yet. But I won't say it couldn't happen.

DP: The Marie Osmond date?

SY: It was a setup. Actually, I'd rather not go into it. (Laughing.)

DP: I want to know.

SY: OK. I'll say this. It was a set-up date and we ended up bowling. We were trying to get to a Jazz game but we ended up bowling.

DP: How were you dressed?

SY: I was under-dressed and I think she was over-dressed.

DP: She had a dress on and you went bowling?

SY: Come on, Dan. **That's as much as I can give you on the Marie Osmond story.**

DP: What are you trying to hide?

SY: I want to protect the innocent.

DP: She's married with six kids.

SY: She's wonderful. She's a friend of mine. And her husband Keith.

DP: So it was love?

SY: No. It was a date. It was a single date.

DP: You know she's a little bit country which would mean that you were a little bit rock and roll.

DP: "Wheel of Fortune."

SY: Two of the most embarassing things in my life were getting beat on "Wheel of Fortune" by **Phil Esposito** and getting beat at the NBA All-Star game in a celebrity three point-shooting contest by Urkel.

DP: You are a sad human being, you know that?

SY: I am.

DP: Everybody would think you have the life. Single. Quarterback of the 'Niners. Making good money. And here you are…a loser.

SY: And bitter!

DP: Urkel kicked your butt.

SY: He hit threes from all over the floor. And you can't find a skinnier guy. I didn't know what to say.

DP: And Phil Esposito owned you. **What did you do to the educational value of a BYU degree?**

SY: I set the whole school back.

DP: And Espo didn't even graduate from high school, did he?

SY: I don't want to hear that.

DP: The Grateful Dead.

SY: I missed the whole thing.

DP: Teri Hatcher.

SY: A fine woman.

DP: Jerry Rice.

SY: A fine receiver.

DP: Brett Favre. And don't say...

SY: A fine quarterback.

DP: Concussions. Do you get tired of people telling you what you should feel about or do with your career because of it?

SY: At the time, I did. I got tired of it. Actually, it brought out a different level in football fans. I had people tell me, "Steve, It's only football. You've got the rest of your life to think about." And these were real, hard-core football fans. Sociologically, I thought it was interesting to get comments like that from football fans.

DP: Does it bother you to see guys celebrating for the sake of celebrating?

SY: What I can't stand is when a guy in my own offense makes a good catch and does that. It screws up the continuity. It's about speed and getting back to the huddle. **It's hard for me to be waiting while some guy does a dance.** We need to get going. But after a touchdown...knock yourself out.

DP: Are you proud of me that we talked for forty minutes and I didn't bring up Joe Montana?

SY: Actually, it doesn't come up that much. After we won the Super Bowl, there was no way to pose an interesting question. **The questions about Joe Montana now are very interesting.** Ones that people have thought about and spent some time on.

DP: I'm amazed that you and Jim McMahon could co-exist.

SY: We got along just fine. Honestly, not that I was any good in college but I was horrible until I got around Jim McMahon and learned how to play football.

DP: No kidding?

SY: Whatever he did, I could copy. And say what you want about him, fundamentally as a football player and a quarterback — awesome. **I became a player because I copied Jim McMahon.**

DAN PATRICK   **TIM DUNCAN**

I don't like Michael Jordan.

im Duncan is quite removed from everything that we think athletes are attached to: stardom, fame, money. He has those things but seems to be more interested in just about everything else. I found him to be candid, refreshing and so mature. I have never been more impressed by an athlete that young.

When we spoke, Tim asked me if I would tell him who was the number-one athlete in the *SportsCentury* list of top athletes of the century. I said I'd tell him if he won the MVP of the NBA Finals. Well, two weeks later he did. And he walks into the interview room, minutes after winning the NBA title, and he just wants me to tell him who the top athlete is. He didn't want to talk about his achievements. He wanted to pick up where we left off.

I couldn't tell him the answer, though. It would ruin the surprise, I said, and my bosses would not be happy if it got out. Oh, yeah. I didn't really know the answer anyway. But I do know this: I am going to be real careful about my next offhand wager with Tim Duncan.

DP: What's your nickname?

TD: The only nickname I have ever had is **Merlin, like the magician.** I don't know why.

DP: You don't know why you're called Merlin?

TD: I kinda know. **I have always been a big Magic Johnson fan.** And I guess the people who knew that gave a name in that...

DP: Respect?

TD: In that vein. I tried to play like him.

DP: So you'd like to run the break?

TD: Absolutely.

DP: Why is it that the big guys want to do what the little guys do and the little guys want to do what the big guys do?

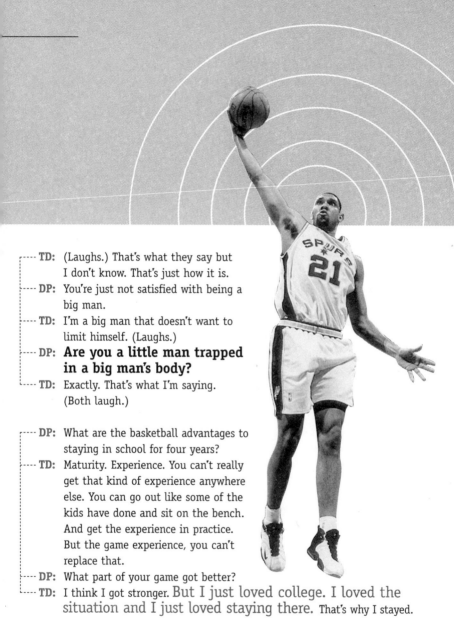

TD: (Laughs.) That's what they say but I don't know. That's just how it is.

DP: You're just not satisfied with being a big man.

TD: I'm a big man that doesn't want to limit himself. (Laughs.)

DP: **Are you a little man trapped in a big man's body?**

TD: Exactly. That's what I'm saying. (Both laugh.)

DP: What are the basketball advantages to staying in school for four years?

TD: Maturity. Experience. You can't really get that kind of experience anywhere else. You can go out like some of the kids have done and sit on the bench. And get the experience in practice. But the game experience, you can't replace that.

DP: What part of your game got better?

TD: I think I got stronger. But I just loved college. I loved the situation and I just loved staying there. That's why I stayed.

DP: Did you endure any rookie hazing?

TD: I got the whole rookies in front of the line to run out for introductions and I'm the only one running out. I got that one.

DP: When did that happen?

TD: My first home game.

DP: Introducing your San Antonio Spurs...

TD: I run out and of course I'm waving and everything. "Hey, everybody!"

DP: It was your San Antonio Spur, singular not plural.

TD: Exactly. **I was an idiot walking out there like that.** (Laughs.)

TD: How's *SportsCenter*? Stop asking me questions. How's *SportsCenter*?

DP: *SportsCenter*'s fine.

TD: Do you like *SportsCenter*?

DP: I have no comment. (Both laugh.) I've been here ten years.

TD: You need to get out, huh?

DP: I'm the Jordan of *SportsCenter*. I told you that.

TD: I know that.

DP: I may retire. If Michael retires, then I am going to retire.

TD: You think you're done, huh?

DP: I could be. I could just go into the clothing business.

TD: The clothing business? You big on clothes?

DP: Just like Jordan. I think I could do that.

TD: You think you got some cologne you can help me out with?

DP: Yeah. **I can help you out with some "Air Patrick" cologne.** (Both laugh.) It's like my game. It stinks.

DP: What opponent taught you the most last year?

TD: **Karl Malone** used a lot of veteran stuff on me that I thought was cool. **Charles Barkley** taught me a lot when I played against him. How he would use his body or use his dribble to get people in there and all that stuff. **Veteran moves.**

DP: Did you ever feel helpless at all last year?

TD: The first game I played against Seattle was the only time I felt destroyed. Vin Baker just manhandled me. The whole thing, their double-teams, their movement, everything. I must have had eight turnovers. Which isn't a big deal for me because **I turn the ball over a lot.** (Laughs.)

DP: I am reading some articles and some of these writers say you never show your personality.

TD: That's what everybody says.

DP: Why is that? What are you hiding?

TD: I'm not hiding anything. **I'm just telling them what they ask.**

If they ask questions, I give them the answers. If we go hang out, that's a whole different thing.

DP: I would see a remarkable change if I talk to you after a game and I went and had beers with you?

TD: Probably more open. More relaxed.

DP: **You're not going to dance on the table?**

TD: That's a possibility. I'm not guaranteeing anything.

DP: Wow. That's good.

DP: Being the **competitive swimmer** that you were, how does swimming compare to basketball?

TD: Swimming is nothing like basketball. Where it has helped me is in training. I go out and work out by myself. But basketball is a team game. And swimming is an individual sport. In one you count on a bunch of guys and in the other you count on yourself.

DP: Admit you were embarrassed putting on the **Speedo.**

TD: **Absolutely not. I have great legs.**

DP: What does your sister Tricia know about you that nobody else knows?

TD: I don't know. She's seen me in a Speedo a lot more than anybody else.

DP: How did you start your **knife collection?**

TD: I have always liked knives. Then somebody gave me one. Then somebody gave me another one. Then I liked having them and started buying them. I started finding ones I liked, ones with funky blades.

DP: Do people give you knives now? If you get married would you get fifty-eight knives for wedding gifts?

TD: I wish. But people don't buy me a whole lot. I've only had six or seven given to me.

DP: The rest you steal?

TD: **I either steal them or carjack somebody and take their knives.** (Both laugh.)

DP: Free association. Favorite TV show.

TD: **"Seinfeld."**

DP: Favorite singers.

TD: Don't have one. I like R&B. I listen to music, not singers.

DP: Favorite celebrity you have met.

TD: Dan Patrick.

DP: Come on.

TD: And Keith Olbermann.

DP: You obviously don't get out much. Favorite celebrity.

TD: You all. Seriously. After David Robinson, it's you all.

DP: That's it? You met Jordan?

TD: But Jordan's Jordan. I have always respected him but I was never the biggest fan of his.

DP: Why aren't you a fan of Jordan's?

TD: Because everybody else is.

DP: Oh, so you don't like Michael Jordan because everybody else does?

TD: No. I don't like Michael Jordan because I don't like Michael Jordan. You got me wrong there. I respect Michael Jordan.

DP: You respect him. You just don't like him.

TD: I'm just somebody that isn't that impressed with him. There really isn't anybody in the world that I am that impressed with.

DP: Do you want to be like Magic?

TD: Yeah.

DP: Why don't you want to be like Larry?

TD: I'd love to be like Larry.

DP: (Laughs.)

TD: It's kind of hard to do.

DP: Isn't it easier to be Larry than Magic?

TD: I don't think so.

DP: You think it's tougher to be Larry than Magic?

TD: Yeah. I have the 6'9" or 6'10" frame down. I'm a black guy. Everything is downhill from there.

DP: But you're not really playing like a black guy are you?

TD: No. Not really.

DP: You just play. You can't jump through the roof.

TD: No.

DP: You're not exceptionally quick.

TD: I'm not … not really.

DP: **Are you a little white man trapped in a big man's black body?**

TD: (Laughs quite a bit.) OK.

DP: Would you agree with that?

TD: Maybe. Not really.

DP: But you see what I am saying?

TD: **I'm not that quick. I play more with my head.**

DP: Yeah.

TD: OK. I'll take that. (Both laugh.)

DP: Give me three young guys you love watching play.

TD: Abdur-Rahim. Stephon Marbury.

DP: I love Stephon Marbury.

TD: Stephon Marbury is the bomb. He is going to be so good. And let's see. I think **Kevin Garnett** is going to be real good at some point. But I think the whole … KG and Kobe Bryant will probably be the guys.

DP: Do you have to win a title to validate how good you are?

TD: Me or people in general?

DP: Both.

TD: Me, I would feel incomplete without it. Other people, I don't think that has to define it. Whether you are a good or a great basketball player.

DP: What would your wrestling name be?

TD: I'd be the … **InTIMidator. That would be my wrestling name.**

DP: What would you wear?

TD: You'd have to incorporate Speedo and Spandex in there.

DP: The InTIMidator wearing a Speedo doesn't really scare people. They'd be doubled over laughing.

TD: That's the trick. It's all a setup. They wouldn't expect it.

DP: I guess they wouldn't. I see.

TD: They'd say that guy's a joke, wearing Speedo and Spandex. While they're laughing, I'd put my finishing move on them. It's over.

DP: I would pay to see that.

TD: **That's what I'm talking about.**

Some nights, I am the best

I once played in a Children's Miracle Network charity softball game with Eric Lindros. As happens with many superstars, I was warned that he didn't have much of a personality. Well, Lindros was on my team, and he couldn't have been more fun. Playing practical jokes, making fun of the other team. I kind of gravitated to him because he was just so much fun to be around.

He made fun of his reputation as a soft player who gets injured too much. He joked about not winning a Stanley Cup yet. I couldn't help but think that if more people, especially the media, could see him in a setting like that, he'd have a different image. I went out of my way to tell the people who had "warned" me about him that he must have had a personality transplant since they saw him. He had a great sense of humor. And of self.

When we spoke, he was the same way. Funny and candid and completely into it. He even asked for more questions when I was winding down. Trust me; *that* was a first.

DP: I'm battling a bad cold here. I may have to be a no-show at work. If it was a pulled groin, I'd play.

EL: Hey, hey — gently. Gently.

DP: Isn't that the worst? People see it in the paper and they know you have a sore groin. Does that bother you?

EL: (Laughs.)

DP: You haven't thought about it much, have you?

EL: I haven't given that much thought to a pulled groin.

DP: It would bother me. "How's your groin?"

EL: It's not something you want to have, but the questions don't bother me.

DP: Are hockey players great athletes?

EL: I'd have to say yes.

player in hockey.

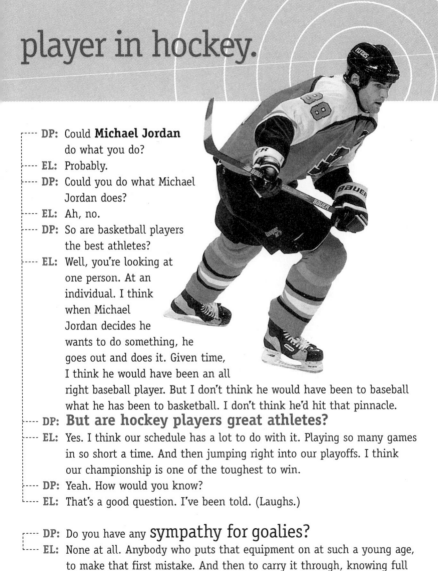

DP: Could **Michael Jordan** do what you do?

EL: Probably.

DP: Could you do what Michael Jordan does?

EL: Ah, no.

DP: So are basketball players the best athletes?

EL: Well, you're looking at one person. At an individual. I think when Michael Jordan decides he wants to do something, he goes out and does it. Given time, I think he would have been an all right baseball player. But I don't think he would have been to baseball what he has been to basketball. I don't think he'd hit that pinnacle.

DP: **But are hockey players great athletes?**

EL: Yes. I think our schedule has a lot to do with it. Playing so many games in so short a time. And then jumping right into our playoffs. I think our championship is one of the toughest to win.

DP: Yeah. How would you know?

EL: That's a good question. I've been told. (Laughs.)

DP: Do you have any **sympathy for goalies?**

EL: None at all. Anybody who puts that equipment on at such a young age, to make that first mistake. And then to carry it through, knowing full well that, "Jeez, it's just not right." I have absolutely no sympathy for him. Not a position I wish to ever, ever take part in.

DP: Three guys you would stay away from in a fight. They drop their gloves but you would rather not go there.

EL: Well, it isn't out of fear but there are situations in which you say, "Why? Why test it?" (Laughs.) **I think if Roger Neilson dropped his gloves, I would avoid him.**

DP: Roger Neilson?

EL: If he dropped his gloves in practice, I would avoid him. We need him. Jeez. Tony Twist has got to be up there. Nah, not Tony Twist. Let's go with Kocur.

DP: Joey Kocur?

EL: Because it only takes one. He's coming with the right and you know it's coming hard.

It's all about avoiding that one punch.

DP: Is there anybody in the league whose ass Wayne could kick?

EL: (Long pause.) I gotta go with the **Beezer.** (Both laugh.) Only because the Beezer has too much equipment up top and he can't come across with his right. (Laughs.)

DP: Does Bacchus do any stupid pet tricks?

EL: He's the god of fine wine and wild behavior. Stupid pet tricks? Well, Bacchus does a lot of sleeping. **He's not a real high energy dog.**

DP: If Bacchus was an NHL player, who would he be?

EL: Kjell Samuelson.

DP: Why is that?

EL: He's a big doof.

DP: Tell me that Journey is not your favorite band.

EL: I don't know where you guys come up with this shit.

DP: Is Journey your favorite band?

EL: No. I am quite definite about that.

DP: I am relieved. When I saw "He likes the band Journey" all I could think of was, "Loving, touching, squeezing." (Laughs.) I couldn't imagine you cuddling up by a fire to that song.

DP: # Favorite hockey name.

EL: Vincent Damphousse. What about Tie Domi? Roman Vopat.
Ron Tugnutt's not bad.

DP: How would you like to go through life named Tugnutt? And have a sore groin.

DP: Can the league afford such high salaries with such limited income?

EL: Who's saying it's limited?
You're owned by Disney. (Laughs.)

DP: Who is the best player in the game?

EL: I think Kariya, Jags, myself. Forsberg.

DP: Anybody else? (Long pause.) Now you're worrying about pissing somebody off by leaving him off.

EL: Not really. That's it. We can stretch this out a long time but if you want the best ... Pick from those four.

DP: But I want your opinion. Are you the best player in hockey?

EL: Some nights I am.

DP: Free association. **The Hanson Brothers.**

EL: "Damn machine stole my quarter." (Both laugh.) "They brought their frickin' toys." "Puttin' on the foil, coach."

DP: I take it you've seen the movie. Hanson the band.

EL: (Long pause.) I have no thought. (Laughs.)

DP: I've stumped you with Hanson?

EL: Well, I'd like to see all six meet.

DP: The Hanson Brothers meet the Hanson Brothers? (Both laugh.) Sports talk radio.

EL: No time for it.

DP: Hockey groupies.

EL: Bored.

DP: I thought you'd say no time for it. The Fox glowing puck.

EL: Zit.

DP: A zit?

EL: A zit. Gotta go.

DP: Do Canadians make fun of Americans, in terms of our ability to play hockey?

EL: No. Give me some more associations. (Laughing.)

DP: OK. 99.

EL: Gretzky.

DP: Terry Murray.

EL: OK, enough associations. (Both laugh.) Florida.

DP: Favorite hockey terms. And you know I have a soft spot for hockey terms.

EL: **The one-timer.** (Both laugh.)

DP: Can you explain the one-timer? It has a sexual connotation to it.

EL: It's a quick pass with a quick release resulting in a tough shot for a goaltender to stop.

DP: Give me three guys you don't want to see on a penalty shot.

EL: Hasek's tough to beat. **Hasek, Cujo and Patty Roy.**

DP: Have you got any questions you'd like me to ask?

EL: You're not a big fan of the one-timer?

DP: I like one-timer. I like top-shelf. I like peanut butter shelf.

EL: Is it peanut butter shelf or going for the peanut butter?

DP: All I know is… What do you think of Barry Melrose's hair?

EL: When you're in my situation… (Both laugh.)

DP: So that's why you like Messier! (Both laugh.)

EL: Listen, I'm not *there* yet.

DP: Is scoring goals overrated?

EL: No. There's a certain amount of elation that goes with every goal. But the celebrating. You know what? I watch the football highlights every Monday morning and we have to work on our celebrating. Apparently, we are not cutting it. Because the highlight ends right after the goal. But with football, the guy crosses the goal line and they give it another five seconds for the dance.

DP: Give me some hockey celebrations.

EL: **Tiger Williams, riding that stick. That's one of the best.**

DP: More.

EL: Like I said, we need help.

DP: **Gretzky's was pretty good, sliding a little bit and thrusting his hand.**

EL: What?

DP: He scored about a thousand goals. Have you seen this?

EL: Jags' salute.

DP: Yeah, but he stole that from the Broncos.

EL: (Slight pause) **I don't think Jags watches football.**

DP: What is the one hockey record that will never be broken?

EL: I think points in a season.

DP: So you think somebody could get Gretzky's 92 goals?

EL: I don't know. Guys have been close. But points...what did he have, 215 or something? **Nobody's going to get near that. There's no way.**

DP: Actresses that you would skip a game to be with?

EL: Well, I wouldn't skip a game.

DP: Maybe skip out of the third period. Three actresses that you would get a gross misconduct penalty for.

EL: **Well, probably Cameron Diaz, Heidi Klum and Carey Lowell.**

DP: What about the rumor that you and Elvis Stojko were in a bar fight? Did he kick your ass?

EL: That was bull. Elvis and I are good friends. Elvis sent out a press release on this. He said it was bullshit.

DP: I was hoping you'd say he kicked your ass. Which would look better in print than "He sent out a press release."

DP: Do you have respect for figure skaters? Could you be one?

EL: No. If you could see my footwork, no. And I don't think I get a whole lot of elevation on my jumps.

DP: But you could wear the outfits?

EL: There are a few, there's some.

DP: I would think you would have a problem with the outfits.

EL: For the most part, but there are a few I could go out on. **It would be a closed-door activity.**

I hear grunts. I hear moans. Every

(B) arry Sanders' agent told me that Jerome Bettis would be a great interview. I wasn't sure one way or the other, but three questions into it, I knew
we would both have some fun—and that I'd learn something.

Bettis was very honest. If I got him with a good question, it was as though
he said "Uncle!" and gave me the answer. It was almost like I was wearing
him down, humorously pounding away at him. He was taking it in the
right way and always had fun. He seemed to realize that I had done some
homework, and he was going to give me the payoff for the effort. A couple
of times he laughed and said, "Where did you get that?" and then
answered the question.

So I pulled the bus off to the side of the road for some repairs. A 5,000-yard
checkup, you might say. And as reluctant as I am to say so, the agent was right.

DP: According to the *Detroit News*, your dad's nickname is Professor Gadget.

JB: Well, you see, he's a nerd. **Pops is a nerd, I must say.** One, he
wears glasses. Two, he has a pocket protector. Three, he rolls up his
sleeves. So, he has all the qualities of a nerd. Although he has those
tendencies, he is a die-hard football fan. But once he goes back to
work, he becomes a nerd again.

DP: Your parents are serious football fans. Do they have any rituals for the
games?

JB: My father likes to wear the same jersey that we wear, the same colors
and everything. Well, he brought the white jersey to Philadelphia this
year and we wore the black jersey. He was ticked off. He was so PO'd
about that he couldn't think straight. And I just laughed at him. I'm
like, "Pops?" He said, "I'm out there with the wrong colors!" He's crazy
about being exactly on point.

now and then, I hear a cry for help.

DP: **When's the last time he spanked you?**

JB: (Laughs.) It's been a while. Since I got bigger than him.

DP: Do you see any of your teammates as being wrestling characters?

JB: Justin Strelczyk would have to be one of those mountain men, I don't know. He's got the big beard going.

DP: He could be Haystacks Calhoun. He wears the bib overalls. Who would you be?

JB: Good question. I'd probably be Ric Flair. The one that everyone loves to hate. When I go into other stadiums, people love to hate me. I get the boos. I get everything.

DP: Is it true that you are only doing this interview because Barry Sanders said something nice about you in an interview with me?

JB: You're a good guy. I love to watch you on *SportsCenter*. When they told me, I said, "It would be an honor." You get interviewed by a lot of stiffs so it's refreshing to be interviewed by someone that you can appreciate.

DP: But when another running back compliments you, is that the best compliment you can receive?

JB: Oh, yes. He knows what I go through.

He knows how I feel on Monday.

DP: Describe your running style.

JB: **Bruising but graceful.** (Both chuckle.)

DP: Would you pull a groin if you tried to run like Barry Sanders?

JB: No question. **I'd break off my ankle. My hips would probably not work anymore. I'd need some artificial joints in order to do some of the things he does.** It's ridiculous when you look at his body, the way he turns and stops and starts. My body couldn't take it. I'd probably just pass out.

DP: I don't think he has any ankles.

DP: When you run into a player, what do you hear?

JB: I hear a lot of grunts. **Sometimes I hear some moans. Every now and then you hear a cry for help.** Those are the ones you appreciate. Because you know that the next time you see him, he's not going to want any part of you.

DP: Would you like to tackle Jerome Bettis?

JB: I wouldn't want to have to do it consistently. It's like riding a rollercoaster. Sure, I'll do it once. I skydived. I'll do it once. I have no problem with that. But if you asked me to get back in that airplane and do it again…

DP: Have you ever been mistaken for Mike Tyson?

JB: Actually, I have. I was in the airport in Phoenix and a middle-aged lady said (in a high-pitched voice), "Is that Mike Tyson?" I looked at her and she said, "Noooo." Yeah, I do get that sometimes and I don't have a problem with it.

DP: You don't have a squeaky voice like he does.

JB: I pride myself on my voice. Keep it as low as I can.

DP: Your nickname in high school was "The Bear." Do you like that better than being called "The Bus?"

JB: I think I like "The Bus" better. Because in high school it was between "The Bear" and my brother called me "Baby Huey."

DP: Oooh, you don't like "Baby Huey."

JB: I didn't like that too much because it meant that I was…

DP: A little chunky?

JB: "Baby Huey" wasn't as derogatory as it sounds. It meant I was the big kid on the block but it just didn't sound good. Bear is like GRRRRR! Grizzly bear. I don't know if that's a great nickname. "The Bus" is a lot better because it can mean a lot more things than "The Bear."

DP: And bus means you can run over somebody or climb on my back and I'll carry you.

JB: **I'm a vehicle of sorts. It can cover a wide variety of things.**

DP: If Walter Payton is Sweetness and you are The Bus, what is Barry Sanders?

JB: **The Magician.**

DP: Terrell Davis.

JB: **Demolition Man.**

DP: What was happening when Coach Cowher ran onto the field and kissed Kordell?

JB: It was like, "You did a great job." And instead of patting him on the back or hitting him on the butt, which is standard…What he did is definitely optional. An optional move, not a recommended situation.

DP: **So would you rather be kissed by Bill Cowher or tackled by Derrick Thomas?**

JB: Tackled by Derrick Thomas. Nine times out of ten if he tackles me, it won't be on the highlights.

DP: But you know if the coach kisses you, we're going to show it!

JB: Exactly. That's going to be all over ESPN.

DP: When you look at coach **Cowher** do you see a player? Do you see a guy who wants to put a uniform on and be with you guys?

JB: When he gets ready for a game, it's the same way we get ready for a game. He has that same strut, same walk and same bounce. You can see it. And it starts in practice. As we go, he goes.

DP: When Kordell Stewart steps into the huddle and says "38 Boss" what do you think?

JB: Here we go. I'm about to make something happen. I want to make sure I read this right because this could be a big one. That's pretty much the only play where I think like that. **But 38 Boss is the one I gear up for. Because if we block it right and I run it right, it can be a big play.**

DP: Could I tell that by the way you approach the line for 38 Boss? That it is your play.

JB: No. Unfortunately I can't tip the defense off that it is my play.

DP: But you never worry that you may be doing that?

JB: Always. Constantly.

DP: Do you look at certain guys and say it's in my best interest to stay away from that guy?

JB: No. My philosophy is that they'll find me.
Nine times out of ten, I'm where the football is. And they're gonna get to the football. We'll run into each other eventually. Those guys love to talk and I love to talk. We have a ball out there. Telling each other what's going to happen.

DP: When is the last time you took a date **bowling?**

JB: Never. You know why? I love to compete. I'm such a competitor that my goal would be to beat the mess out of her. And I would tell her, "I'm going to beat your butt." And after I beat her butt I would tell her, "You're terrible because I beat your butt." **I think it would destroy the relationship before it got started.**

DP: Give me the defensive player who needles you the most about your nickname. Talking smack on your nickname.

JB: **Every team we play, all I hear is, "The Bus ain't going nowhere today."** I never know who says it because I'm at the bottom of the pile.

DP: Free association. The Temptations.

JB: Women.

DP: Earl Anthony.

JB: 300.

DP: **Rocky Balboa.**

JB: (As Stallone) **"Adrienne."**

DP: **Kordell Stewart.**

JB: **Slash.**

DP: Bill Cowher.

JB: The chin. (Much laughter.) You're going to get me in trouble.

DP: Lou Holtz.

JB: Motivator.

DP: In a national poll this summer, sports fans said tackling Jerome Bettis was the scariest thing in sports.

JB: That's an honor, I think. If you consider everything in sports...

DP: Do you consider it the scariest thing in sports?

JB: No.

DP: What is scarier than tackling you?

JB: **I think an 85-miles-an-hour curveball that is coming at your head.** I don't know how you can hit that because you're not thinking about the ball at that point. You're thinking about getting out of the way. Hitting a curveball by some of these pitchers is scarier than me running down their throats.

DP: I think I'd rather try tackling you than face <u>Randy Johnson.</u>

JB: Exactly.

DP: If he hits me in the head, I die. You hit me, OK, I'm in the hospital for a little while.

JB: Maybe you lose a spleen.

DP: But I'm still breathing.

DAN PATRICK   **ROGER CLEMENS**

The ball had bad intentions

® oger Clemens was perhaps the most self-conscious of the athletes I have interviewed for the magazine. He seemed very measured about what he was going to say. He didn't want to hurt anybody's feelings. He called me back later to take a fairly innocuous remark about another pitcher off the record. He really wanted to be politically correct.

It's tough to admit this but I don't think I got to him. Based on my standard of trying to reveal a new side to each subject, I don't think I did a great job. I still think the interview is interesting, and Roger and I did have some fun, but I don't think he ever relaxed and just chatted with me. I think he remained "Roger Clemens, pitcher." I was looking for "Roger Clemens, human being." He was generous with stories about other people but he held back for the most part about himself. He was starting his second year with the Blue Jays when we spoke, so maybe that situation affected him. Or maybe he is just gun-shy with the press from all those years in Boston, where the media can be brutal. I don't know. I like the guy and would welcome the opportunity to talk again.

Clemens did give me one remarkable insight on how he competes. Next time I want ten of those, Roger.

DP: We'll just fire away here. Best assumed name you've checked into a hotel under.

RC: Ferris Bueller.

DP: Why'd you pick him?

RC: I don't know. Actually, they messed it up and I became Festus. So everybody called me Festus. Or Bueller.

DP: This is a science though, isn't it? You guys take great pride in having a great assumed name, don't you?

RC: Well, not really. I've never really used one. The pranksters think it's

for sure.

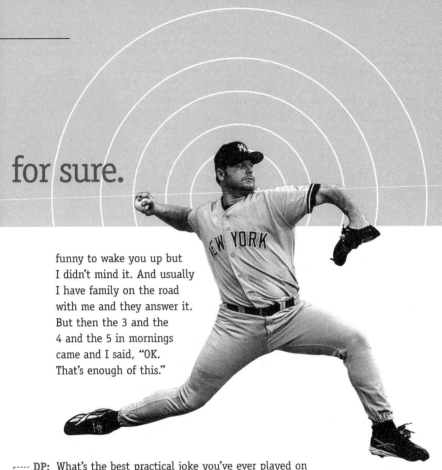

funny to wake you up but I didn't mind it. And usually I have family on the road with me and they answer it. But then the 3 and the 4 and the 5 in mornings came and I said, "OK. That's enough of this."

DP: What's the best practical joke you've ever played on a teammate?

RC: Probably the one I played on **Ellis Burks. Goldie Hawn** was in Boston making *House Guest* with Steve Martin. She and **Kurt Russell** came to the park one night and after the game we all were hanging around. Ellis comes over and says, "I want his autograph, too. What should I say?" I told him to just go over and make small talk. Then I said, "When he's signing your ball, tell him you loved him in the movie *Ghost*." Russell gave him a real sarcastic "Ha Ha Ha." A few weeks later, Paul Newman was at the park and, **on his own, Ellis called him Robert Redford. Newman didn't think it was that funny.**

DP: Do you have to be a great athlete to be a pitcher?

RC: At this level, **you have to be a great athlete to do anything.**

DP: As a fraternity, you try to stick up for your fellow pitchers. But give me a physique you wouldn't wish on anybody.

RC: I don't want to hoot on anybody.

DP: There's not an active pitcher that you would say, "God did not want him to be a pitcher with that physique?" **David Wells?**

RC: I just saw Boomer today. He looked good. I guess the Boss must have been getting on him a little bit. He's looking better than he did this time last year.

DP: Hideki Irabu?

RC: I saw him today but only for a little bit.

DP: Don't give me this politically correct stuff. God.

DP: Three guys who had no business hitting home runs off of you.

RC: All three would be Andy Allanson. The guys in Cleveland, they never let me live that one down. And my brother-in-law swears that Jeff Frye took me deep but I can't picture it. Would you look that up for me? I might owe him a hundred bucks.

DP: You forget who hits home runs off you?

RC: No. I'm saying I would remember it. If French Frye hit a home run off me, I would know it.

DP: Andy Allanson?

RC: He one-handed a slider that hit the top of the pad in old Cleveland Stadium, right by the foul pole in left field. **The guys hammered me so hard that I just should have taken my jersey off and kept walking. It was that bad.**

DP: Who was the last guy you intentionally hit?

RC: I think it was **Tim Salmon.**

DP: Why would you hit a nice guy like Tim Salmon?

RC: I give him a lot of respect. It wasn't meant to hit him, it was just an inside fastball. But it had bad...

DP: Intentions?

RC: Yeah. **I think the ball had bad intentions for sure.**

DP: Defend the designated hitter.

RC: I don't know that I'd want to. The only way that I could would be in an inter-league game. You come out after a 70-pitch performance. I'd feel like I didn't do my job. I know they had to make a change and put a hitter in for me, a chance to score runs. But to get pulled after 70 pitches ... you don't even feel like icing your arm. I tease guys like Greg Maddux who have a complete game with 82 pitches. I tell him I'd fine him for putting his stuff in the wet bag. There's no way he could have sweated. But then he says if he had a frame like me or Smoltz, he would never get sore.

DP: Give me a pitcher you would be afraid to hit against.

RC: Randy Johnson, definitely. Also Gibson or Drysdale or Nolan Ryan. Those guys would come after you if you took too long to get in the box.

DP: What's your most prized piece of sports memorabilia?

RC: A ball autographed by Cy Young that a friend gave me. Now, when I was a rookie, I thought it was interesting to meet the older players on Old-Timers' Day. Especially when I was in Boston and all these great guys would be in the clubhouse. I was too young and green to approach Bob Gibson and Warren Spahn. Ted Williams, Luis Tiant. DiMaggio. One day, I was getting dressed and there was a guy in a wheelchair. We end up talking for half an hour. I got up to leave and said good-bye. Our public relations director came over and said, "Do you know who that was you were talking to?" I had no idea. **"That was Joe Wood."** There was one of the great ones. He won three World Series games, I think, in one Series. I got an old cancelled check signed by him that I really, really like.

DP: I know that two years ago in Texas you were charting pitches one day and you asked Aaron Sele to take over so **you could bid on JFK's golf clubs.** You had to be nervous.

RC: I got permission to do it. We had some idea of when it would start and then it got completely blown out of the water. Of course, the guys are egging me on. They wanted me to go crazy.

DP: Those clubs went for about $367,000, didn't they?

RC: Yeah. I thought I would go to $121,000, 21 being our number. It hovered around $80,000 for a while so I took it over $100,000. Then it went up to $130,000 and it just spiraled to two, 250, 300. And, not being there, on the phone, I just bailed on it. To have his bag or his clubs, that would be a good piece of history.

DP: Would you buy Bill Clinton's clubs?

RC: Probably not.

DP: Why not?

RC: **When I see highlights, he's not hitting 'em straight.** (Laughter.)

DP: What role does fear play in baseball?

RC: It depends on the individual. Early in my career, it was fear of the unknown, of what it was going to take to make it. Fear might be too strong a word, though, when it comes to a batter and a pitcher. **Respect is probably a better word and I think I've earned it.**

DP: Can you sense fear? Or nervousness?

RC: You've got to be nervous to get that adrenaline going. With me, **I try to beat you three ways.** Physically, I'm going to try to beat you and I know I've done everything to prepare. If that's failing, my mental game has to go to a new level. And if those two fail, I go to emotions. And I know I play on emotions as much as the other two. I'll say something to a teammate or an opposing player that I probably shouldn't. I'll think about my mother's sickness. **I'll think about my grandmother who passed on. Whatever it takes to elevate my game if I know I'm lethargic out there, I'll do it.**

DP: Would you love to hit a ball four hundred feet?

RC: I do with my driver, out on the course. But I've had my at-bats and gotten a few knocks. I've been pretty lucky.

DP: You aren't pretty up there.

RC: I had all that catcher's gear on. That's a farce too. Going up the with all that armor on. If you get hit, you should be able to feel it. And it ought to hurt a little bit.

DP: Three pitchers that you have taken something from and put it in your arsenal.

RC: **Nolan Ryan's explosion stage** from his lower half from when I used to sneak into the Astrodome just to watch him warm up. His mound presence, too. **I watched Tom Seaver's leg drive** and his mechanics to control the ball and his ability to throw a fastball to nine different locations. That gives you nine different pitches if you throw them in different areas. I played with Tom in Boston and **when he talked I was like a sponge.** I talked to **Don Drysdale** about power and about having a passion about what you're doing. To pitch inside and not give in.

DP: One hitter that you'd love to face that you never have.

RC: Mickey Mantle, Babe Ruth. Now that you mention it, Dan, I would also have liked to pitch to Bench and Fisk.

DP: Give me the other two guys that shouldn't have hit one off you?

RC: Well, anybody who has a bat could do it BUT....

DP: Somebody with no business...

RC: **I'm just glad I didn't give up the one off of Jose Canseco's head.** We tease Jose about what he and Michael Jackson have in common... **one glove for no apparent reason.**

I want to get down and dirty.

hen I saw Keyshawn Johnson play at USC, I thought he was the best football player in the country. I told him that at an ESPN function after the season. He returned the compliment about my work and later mentioned me in his book as one of the few sports journalists that he admires. So we do have a little history.

I like his attitude and his spirit. Keyshawn has a drive that is remarkable for a kid who had such a difficult upbringing. He has been fighting all his life. The scrappiness that you see on the football field is not anything new for him. He's not taking anything for granted. Keyshawn's bottom line is winning games, not compiling statistics. He can play on any team I'm putting together.

After his book came out, I defended Keyshawn a bit. So he wants the ball? Big deal. Pete Rose was selfish but won more baseball games than anybody. Michael Jordan was selfish but he was selfish about winning. If you have the talent, if you can get us the win, go ahead and ask for the ball. I don't mind that at all. It's certainly preferable to the guys who don't want the damn ball.

DP: Do you still feel like a Raider or a Raider-type player? You once told me that you wished you had been drafted by them. Do you think you'll end up there?

KJ: I was brought up on watching and following the Raiders by living in Los Angeles. I wasn't a Lamb fan. It was USC. It was the Coliseum. It was the whole Marcus Allen thing. Their home stadium was across the street from where I grew up. My attitude fit that image of a Raider. When I look at myself on a football field, I see myself as a nasty receiver. **I play like a wide receiver that's a linebacker.** I'll block. All that attitude, to me, is a Raider attitude.

I see myself as a nasty receiver.

DP: Do you think your **attitude** is sometimes misinterpreted?

KJ: I think it all comes from my rookie year. I just wanted to win so bad. I don't think people had seen that attitude before. They were used to shy people who just say what you're supposed to say. Textbook. They tell you what to say in college. What to say at the combine. What to say at the Heisman ceremony. What to say when they draft you. You say A, B and C. Never go to D, E and F. **If you do that, you're not doing what we want.** Ever since then people have wanted to find a way to find a niche for whatever I do or say.

DP: Do you wish you hadn't written that book?

KJ: Oh, no. Not at all. But I don't think under these circumstances, with this coach that I'm dealing with, that the book would have come out anywhere near the way it did. I wouldn't have been talking about a 1-15 season. I wouldn't have been talking about being used unfairly. And I definitely wouldn't have been talking about a quarterback that didn't seem to care. If I played with Parcells as a rookie, I would have been talking about a Super Bowl. (Laughs.)

DP: Give me a defensive back in the AFC East **that you have the most respect for?**

KJ: **Ty Law.** I like Ty Law a lot. I don't know him as an individual but I respect his game. I don't think he gets the respect he deserves. He's physical and I've seen him run with the best of them. I just like the overall toughness in his play.

DP: Who else?

KJ: I like **Terrell Buckley** a lot. I like his enthusiasm. Both those guys are fun to watch play.

DP: Is racism still attached to the quarterback position?

KJ: I don't think so. I just think there aren't enough African-American quarterbacks out there. But the ones that are get the opportunity, I think they get a fair chance. Like Steve McNair. Tony Banks. Wally Richardson. As long as they produce, I think they get a fair opportunity. Look at Donovan McNabb. Look at Daunte Culpepper. There's no reason they won't play on Sunday.

DP: Should the NFL go out of its way to **protect quarterbacks?**

KJ: I'm standing around getting beaten up, too. Are they going out of their way to protect receivers?

DP: Should they wear skirts or a special jersey?

KJ: If they're going to complain about getting hit all the time, then they probably should. Seriously. **Because if they wear a skirt, then I'm going to wear one too.** As much punishment as I take...

DP: What's a story you'll tell your children about Bill Parcells?

KJ: Last year in the Giants game. I dropped one pass. He says to me on the sidelines, "How many'd you drop? How many do you think you dropped? How many? Four? Five?" I said, "Oh, probably just 2." "Yeah, right. It looked like six to me." But that's OK. My rookie year nobody would have said anything to me but the next thing you know, they would stop throwing to me. Or I'd be out of the game.

DP: Are there guys in the game you would sit and watch play?

KJ: Michael Irvin. Jerry Rice. Cris Carter. Barry Sanders. Jerome Bettis. Emmitt Smith.

DP: So you're a football fan?

KJ: Oh, yeah. I go to high school games on Fridays when I can.

DP: Give me the three best talkers you know in the NFL.

KJ: Corey Fuller. Ty Law. Thomas Smith. From Buffalo. Terrell Buckley's in there too. He's taking every route to the house. And that's just the joy of playing football. Being able to have fun and believe in your ability to get it done.

DP: Do you have a hard time not talking in the huddle?

KJ: **I talk in the time-outs.** I talk when I want the ball in crucial situations. I say, "Glenn, one on one, look for cover three." I give him the huddle because he's the general. In the time-outs I talk to the offensive line. Last year John Randle was going on one of his tirades. And I asked Jumbo Elliott, "Does he scare you?" And he just gave me a look and smiled.

DP: Do you make fun of Parcells behind his back?

KJ: **You're gonna get me cut!**
(Laughs.) But people seem to think I'm the best coach impersonator we have. I pretty much have everybody down pat. I don't make fun of him. I mimic him. When he's not around. It's in fun.

DP: You don't make fun of his physique?

KJ: No. He's an older guy. **He's not gonna have a Mr. Universe body at that age.**

DP: Is it hard for today's black athlete to relate to an older, white coach?

KJ: No. I don't think it is. He's had inner-city, urban black players before. Carl Banks. Pepper Johnson. Lawrence Taylor. Joe Morris. John Robinson too. Lou Holtz. They've had contact with young black players before. Chip Banks, Willie McGinest. It's an understanding. These are older guys who have had run-ins with younger players but all of these guys have won. So they are well respected in that manner. When you get a guy who hasn't won a damn thing coming in and thinking he's the next Tommy Lasorda or Pat Riley, that's when you have a problem with him as a young athlete, not a black athlete.

DP: It sounds like you have had these thoughts before.

KJ: I've only ever had one coach in my life where I said to myself, "He's a nice guy but I don't think he knows what he's doing."

DP: Who?

KJ: Richie Kotite. I was never concerned about Bill Parcells that way or John Robinson. He had a fine career in the NFL with the Rams. It's not his fault Eric Dickerson wanted all that money. It wasn't Bill Parcells' fault we were 1-15. He was at the Super Bowl, drinking champagne. I respected him even before he was my head coach. Athletes have problems with coaches who can't coach.

Every athlete who has a problem with a coach is on a team that sucks.

What athlete that you know of, when they're winning, has a problem with the coach?

DP: Free association. **Tupac Shakur.**

KJ: A rebel.

DP: **Kenneth Starr.**

KJ: I don't even know who the hell Kenneth Starr is. I don't watch it. I believe Clinton. I'm going down with Clinton. That's all I'm saying.

DP: Careful how you say that. Should President Clinton resign?

KJ: I don't know enough about it to make a comment.

DP: **Spike Lee.**

KJ: Role model.

DP: **Chris Rock.**

KJ: Comedian. Everything he does is funny. He came to my party and made me laugh by just looking at him.

DP: **Wayne Chrebet.**

KJ: I don't know. I can't describe him in one word.

DP: You can use a couple.

KJ: **Over-achiever.** Because he's over-achieved, basically.

DP: Has your relationship with him improved?

KJ: My relationship with him is the same as it's always been. It never went up or down.

DP: Is he a friend or a teammate?

KJ: He's more of a teammate. A friend is someone you deal with outside of football, outside of your team. I've been asked this a million times. **He's a teammate of mine.** I don't call Wayne Chrebet and ask him if I can drive his car to Washington, D.C. because I don't have oil in mine. I might with Richie Anderson. Or Chris Hayes. Or Aaron Glenn.

DP: Given your head coaches with the Jets, who's the better athlete?

KJ: Well, there's only been two.

DP: Who then?

KJ: Parcells, I guess.

DP: You think Parcells could handle **Kotite?** Richie was a pretty decent tight end.

KJ: I didn't know that. I didn't know he played in the NFL. That's a shame. That's the type of information I got. When I played for him, I did not know that he played in the NFL. Until you said that.

DP: No kidding.

KJ: Swear to god.

DP: You didn't try to get to know him?

KJ: They didn't try to get to know me.

DP: Have you ever tried steroids?

KJ: I'm 180 pounds. What the hell would steroids help me at?

DP: Get you up to 200.

KJ: I have never had the opportunity or desire. I've got skills. I don't need that stuff. **I don't need stuff to help me dominate you when I'm going to dominate you anyway.**

DP: I like to hear that.

Brett Hull says all the things

(W)ayne Gretzky and I sat down together in Boston in the spring of 1999. He had not yet announced his retirement, but I felt something was different. I mentioned that I had a few different things to cover, a "Sunday Conversation" and the magazine. Gretzky just said go as long as you want. He too may have sensed it was sort of a last roundup.

In the fall of 1999, I spent part of a weekend with Gretzky in South Bend, Indiana, for the USC–Notre Dame game. He totally let his guard down. He was ragging on me, having fun and displaying a wicked sense of humor. He also told me that he did not want to be number one on the *SportsCentury* list because he just didn't need the pressure and the attention. (Michael Jordan said the same thing.)

First of all, Gretzky is one of about five people for whom that statement is not a joke, but it also told me how savvy he is. He said he wanted to be two, four or nine. Second-best athlete of the century. Or in the top five. Or top ten. He didn't want the top spot, but he knew his place was near it. Hard to argue with that.

DP: Who was your mentor or hero as a kid?

WG: Like most Canadian kids, **Gordie Howe was my ultimate hero.** It was funny because I got to meet Gordie when I was 10 years old. For most kids, or most people, you meet your hero and you think, "Oh, he's really not that nice or he's really not that good." For me it was the opposite. He was bigger and better than I ever could have imagined. I spent the rest of my childhood thinking that one day I hope I can be as good a hockey player as Gordie Howe.

I wish I could say.

DP: What were your thoughts about Michael Jordan, his last year and when he retired?

WG: I thought that he would continue to play and almost selfishly as a parent you say, **"You just can't leave our kids like that!"** (Laughter.)

DP: Did you look at him and say, "That's how I want to handle it?"

WG: Hey listen, every single athlete gets up in the morning and says the way it's going to end is to score the last goal in overtime or sink the last basket or run in the last touchdown like John Elway did.
We all would love to ride off into the sunset like that.

DP: Is Jordan the Gretzky of the NBA or are you the Jordan of the NHL?

WG: No. **Jordan is the Jordan of sports.** I don't think there is any athlete, maybe with the exception of Muhammad Ali, who has done and contributed to his sport like he has done. Maybe Babe Ruth but no one else is in that category.

DP: Did part of you not want to break Gordie Howe's records?

WG: No. I don't think that way at all. And I'm very proud of everything I've done, but I'd be the first guy there to shake someone's hand if they were to break my records.

DP: Is it tough being The Great One every night?

WG: I suppose but my approach comes from my dad. I was 10 years old and I scored 378 goals that year. We played the very last game of the year but nobody really wanted to play. Well, we went to this little town and they sold out the place. There's like 2,000 people in this old barn kind of arena. We got beat 7-1 and I remember I got in the car and I was kind of smiling. All of a sudden I could see my dad's face. He finally turned to me and he said, "You know you can't do that. Even though you're 10 years old, you have to be ready to play every single game because people are coming to see you. You've created this image that you're this guy and you cannot take days off." I looked at my dad and said, "Ah, you're crazy." (Laughter.) Like my kids say to me now. But it was probably one of the greatest lessons I've ever had. Now, I have had bad games, I'm human, but I am always mentally and physically prepared to play.

DP: What's up with Barry Melrose's hair?

WG: I was doing a video shoot three days ago for my clothing line. I said, "Oh, I'll just trim my hair a little bit." Next thing I know I walk out and my wife says, "What happened to your hair?" I said, "I don't know. I look like Barry Melrose." (Laughter.)

DP: When do you feel old?

WG: Fifteen years ago. (Laughter.)

DP: Do you ever put on the goalie equipment?

WG: My kids always say, "Daddy, get in goal." Have a little more respect for me than that. (Laughter.)

DP: Have you ever had sympathy for a goalie?

WG: Never. Well, I guess I did one time and I got myself into trouble. An old teammate was playing in New Jersey. We got 13 goals on him and I went public and said some silly things about New Jersey. I was young and it was wrong to say. But I said it and I said it because I felt bad for him. That's the only reason I said it.

DP: Do you wonder what you would have been like 15 years ago if back then you thought about the game the way you do now?

WG: That's life, though. I'm a different player at 38 than I was at 23. Part of my success in the '80s was because the game was faster and more open. There was more space on the ice and there was a lot more goal scoring. But I put myself in a tough position. I'm always compared to Wayne Gretzky at a younger age. And that's the toughest part of being me.

DP: Does it still hurt what happened in the Olympics, not being picked for the shoot-out?

WG: No. There was more of a deal made of it by other people than by me. It was so funny. Now if you've played in overtime you are not nervous — obviously you have anxiety — but you are not nervous because you are playing. But all of a sudden they say, "You're not shooting." You become a fan and your nerves take over to the point where you can't watch. I almost wanted to walk into the locker room. Joey Nieuwendyk was sitting beside me and he asked me three times where should he shoot on Hasek. Finally he says, "You don't have anything to say, do you?" And I said, **"Joey, I can't talk!"** (Laughter.)

DP: Favorite hockey term?

WG: There was an old hockey announcer named Danny Gallivan, on **"Hockey Night in Canada,"** that had all these different sayings. One of the things that he used to say was, "That was a Savardian-like move." He meant Serge Savard, who'd fake in and do a "spin-a-rama" move.

DP: Is it the game that still brings a smile to your face or is it just competing? Because there is a difference between enjoyment and competition.

WG: I think for me the competition is the fun. Because if I wasn't playing here I don't think that I would play pick-up hockey. I mean I love the game, but I'm not a guy who's going to play Thursday night hockey when I'm done. That's not for me.

DP: Who was the last guy to ask you for an autograph?

WG: Who was the last guy to ask me for an autograph? Your son. (Laughter.) Half an hour ago!

DP: No, no, no. A player.

WG: I don't mean to brag but in every locker room before a game there is a training table full of sweaters, sticks, pucks and pennants that teams want signed. So to narrow it down to which guy it actually was would be hard. **I guess Vincent Lecavalier was probably the last guy who actually came over and asked me.**

DP: Is it strange when somebody asks?

WG: No, because I did it all the time. I played with **Gordie Howe** when I was 17. Jacques Demers picked me to be on that team. I couldn't believe that I got picked to play. I remember all I kept thinking was, "How am I going to get his stick?" I wasn't real concerned about the game. I kept thinking that I need to get a signed stick. And I did it. And as time went on I played with Guy LeFleur in the Canada

Cup and I asked for his stick. You find that all the hockey players, at least all the ones that I played with, and that's almost all of them, are really nice and if a guy asks me for a stick—not a problem.

DP: Aside from your family, what is the one thing that you would take into the millennium?

WG: A Gordie Howe stick from 1947 that I got in a trade.

DP: Who would you consider colorful, Dennis Rodman-like, in the NHL?

WG: Not Dennis Rodman-like, Charles Barkley-like. Brett Hull. (Laughter.)

DP: He's the Charles Barkley of the NHL?

WG: I always told him, **"Hull, you say all the things that I wish I could say."**

DP: What's the strangest thing that you have ever done with the

Stanley Cup?

WG: I don't think that there was anything strange that we did, because when we won it we had so much respect for it. One time I put it in the trunk of my car. I was going from house to house in Edmonton. When you win a championship, everyone is so happy for you and so excited to be part of it. So I said, **"You want to see the Cup?"** They said "Yeah, where is it?" I said, **"It's in the trunk."** "In the TRUNK?" (Laughter.) I flipped the guy my keys and said, **"Go get it."**

DP: Well, I took a sip out of the cup that the Rangers won. And I remember saying to Messier, "What's in it?" And he said if you have to ask...

WG: Well, that's one thing I will tell you. I've only sipped it one time. (Laughter.)

DP: No telling where it's been.

WG: Sipping ... That's not a wise thing to do.

DAN PATRICK   **JEFF GORDON**

On the race track, size

Ⓗe is Cola-Cola. He is IBM. He is AT&T. Jeff Gordon is a conglomerate. He's also a clean-cut kid who didn't grow up on a country dirt road. He doesn't know everything there is to know about what goes on under the hood of his car. He's a polite and successful, well-dressed businessman with a beautiful wife. He just happens to drive a car for a living. And, like those big corporations, he usually wins. As a result, it's easy to dislike him.

To his credit, he understands that he doesn't fit the image of the classic NASCAR hero. He offers no apologies for it. He knows what he's doing. In a way, that attitude is right in step with any legendary driver you could name: Take me as I am. We keep waiting for him to change, though, to be like everybody else. I don't think he should. It's working.

When I called him, he was in his office signing some autographs. I understood immediately how I fit into his day, where my slot was. Usually, these interviews run a bit longer than scheduled because they are fun and informal. But Jeff pretty much had to go when he said he had to go. Business as usual.

DP: What's the strangest fan autograph you've received?

JG: Oh, man. I've had some strange ones. One of the strangest ones I've ever done, and I've had a couple people do this, **they want me to sign either their arm or the top of their shoulder so they can get it tattooed in.** (Both laugh.)

DP: That's kind of scary.

DP: I would guess that would make you a Jeff Gordon fan for life. You wouldn't want to change and say I'm now a Hud Stricklin fan.

JG: There are people with half of their backs that have number 24 and Rainbow colors and Jeff Gordon on it. I think, "What happens if

doesn't matter.

I change sponsors or numbers?" They say they'll get it changed. I'm like, "Oh, my goodness." **Those type of people definitely scare me.**

DP: You guys don't have just an audience. You have people who live and die with each driver.

JG: There are some people out there who are just fans of the sport and just like everything about it. But then there are some who are so dedicated that they just eat, sleep and drink this stuff. It's their whole life. I've got people that basically buy souvenirs, those die-cast cars and things, to support their kids when they go to college. They tell me they're going to sell these things one day. I just say, "Okaaaay."

DP: Do you think if you looked differently the old school NASCAR would accept you a little bit more?

JG: I think there are several things that contribute to all of this. When I grew up in racing, my family put interviews and the way I handled myself in front of the TV camera and around sponsors as an important part of it and making driving important also. So when I got to NASCAR and started winning races, those other things get critiqued because they're used to a good ol' boy saying whatever's on his mind and not always doing the right thing, you know?

DP: Well, if you could do it differently...

JG: **I wish I had spent more time working with the cars.** As I grew up, my step-dad wanted me to work on the cars and earn my way up through the ranks. And with the sprint cars it's a very simple car so it's fairly easy to learn these cars. So I kind of knew these cars as I was growing up but when I got into Busch Grand National and NASCAR, I knew nothing about a full-bodied stock car. I know a lot about the cars now but it has taken me a lot longer because I am focusing on driving. But do I really know it like the guys on my team? No, I don't. Or other drivers or other guys out there? Like Rusty Wallace; he knows every aspect of that car. I think that would probably help earn me a little more respect.

DP: What is the hardest job in the pit crew?

JG: The one that I could not do is jacking the car. I just physically could not do it. We've got one-pump jacks these days so you need a mass of about 230 pounds just to get that thing down. I know I couldn't possibly do that. It would be tough to change the right front tire. That guy runs around first. And if that car comes in there and slides over that line, he's the first guy to get hit.

DP: What is the best racing movie?

JG: What was the one **Steve McQueen** did? *Grand Prix*? That was a pretty good one.

DP: *Days of Thunder?*

JG: I like the movie because I like Tom Cruise and Nicole Kidman. And Jerry Bruckheimer. But the movie wasn't realistic. Good movie, just not realistic.

DP: Were you Tom Cruise in that movie?

JG: (Laughs.) I get called Cole every once in a while. But I don't ride a Harley. No, I think that was Tim Richmond.

DP: **OK. So it wasn't Dick Trickle?**

JG: It was his long-lost cousin.

DP: If your work car had a CD player in it, what would it be playing during a race?

JG: Probably Will Smith. **"Getting Jiggy Wit' It."**

DP: I didn't expect that out of you but....

JG: I like all kinds of different music. I turn on the Top 40 station and whatever comes on...Ricky Martin.

DP: Oh, no!

JG: I am getting kind of sick of that. (Both laugh.)

DP: You're not living **"La Vida Loca."** Do you ever sing during a race? I know it's intense but have you ever found yourself singing or humming?

JG: **In the shower on race day I'll sing, "I'm gonna win this race." A little Elvis.** (Both laugh.)

DP: <u>Are race car drivers athletes?</u>

JG: Is a marathon runner an athlete? Because I consider us going 500 miles sort of like a marathon runner. It's not purely physically demanding as though you were lifting 200 or 300 pounds on a bench press. But your neck goes through a lot of G-forces and **by the end of the race it's hard just to hold your neck up.**

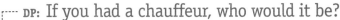

DP: If you had a chauffeur, who would it be?

JG: Nobody. Me. I would put the hat on and the tux or whatever and get in the limo. I don't like anybody to drive me.

DP: You wouldn't trust anybody? Another NASCAR driver?

JG: There are two ways to do this. As a chauffeur or I'm riding in the right seat of their race car. If you throw Earnhardt into the driver's seat, he's purposely going to try to scare the heck out of you. He's going to run into the wall a few times just to do it. I wouldn't want him. Probably Dale Jarrett or Mark Martin. I think Mark Martin is the kind of guy who is very talented but yet in total control and safe. **Earnhardt is all those things but he's a little wild.**

DP: I thought you might say Michael Jordan. Or Mark McGwire.

JG: How about **Joe Montana?**

DP: You think he'd be in complete control?

JG: Absolutely. Precise. He would map out the whole route and know exactly where he has to turn. He's got it together. He's got a plan.

DP: What do you think of baseball toying with the idea of putting ads on the uniforms?

JG: I think they're stealing it from us.

(Laughs.) They're seeing NASCAR's popularity growing and the sponsors so attracted to NASCAR and seeing all those logos. And five years ago people used to laugh at us. "Man, look at the uniforms you guys have. Look at all those logos all over the place. What's up with that?" Now, you have people saying, "Man, how do we do that?"

DP: Are people curious about **potty breaks** for you guys?

JG: That's the second most frequently asked question.

DP: That's what I thought. So, 500 miles…Is there a delicate way to answer that question?

JG: It really is amazing how mind over matter works. I can remember times when it was real hot and I'm drinking a lot of fluids. Then I'm in the car buckling up and I say, "Oh, no! I have to go right now. How am I going to make it the whole race?" And an hour after the race I'm like, "Oh, yeah. I have to go to the bathroom."

DP: What is the first thing to go on a driver?

JG: Their hearing. (Laughs.)

DP: But when does it start to go downhill?

JG: I think you definitely lose that edge a little bit. You see these young guys in our sport and they are just bustin' off these laps. Getting poles and early in the race they are driving by guys and just flying. You think, "Well, they'll learn." **One of these days when they are a bit older, they'll hit a wall. They'll learn. They won't drive quite like that anymore.** You'll see guys putting it on the edge and driving sideways. After a few walls, you drive a bit different, smarter. You say, "I'll save it for when I need it."

DP: Free association. **Dale Earnhardt.**

JG: Ummmm. Tough. (Laughs.)

DP: **Benny Parsons.**

JG: Great commentator.

DP: **Tom Cruise.**

JG: Icon.

DP: **Austin Powers.**

JG: Hilarious.

DP: **Tony Stewart.**

JG: Great talent.

DP: **Have you ever been scared?**

JG: Oh, yeah. Every weekend.

DP: Are you truly scared?

JG: **Absolutely. Every weekend.** That's what keeps you from going over the edge. We literally put the cars on the edge every single weekend. When we're going to qualify, we basically start out with somewhat of a tight setup. And we just loosen up, loosen up, loosen up. And then all of a sudden, we go boom, wiggle, car gets sideways. We go,

"Oh, boy, that was close."

And I guarantee you at that moment, I am scared. And I say, "OK, guys, we have to back it off from there." There are also times when the car jumps out from underneath you or a wreck happens right in front of you. That instant fear is there. If you deny it, then you are lying to yourself.

DAN PATRICK   DOUG FLUTIE

I do love proving

Even after he washed out with the Patriots and Bears and headed for the Canadian Football League, I still thought Doug Flutie could play in the NFL. Eventually, he came back to lead the Bills to a great year in 1998 and is still going strong, but that Canadian exile gave him a chip on his shoulder that drives him to this day.

Flutie remembers anyone who ever wrote or said something negative about him. I think he needs the constant motivation that is provided by the people who tell him what he can't do. I am glad he has kept at it because we need people like Doug Flutie to remind us of what is possible in sports. We tend to label people quickly, and if he had accepted his label we would all have been cheated out of some pretty special moments. It is no stretch to say that his CFL/NFL numbers are of Hall of Fame quality.

In the same way that Pete Sampras uses the idea that he is boring as motivation, Flutie uses the endless references to his height. But Sampras laughs it off because he knows it isn't true. Flutie, who is aware of how tall he is, bristles because he knows it doesn't matter.

DP: Best thing about the rules in **Canadian football.**

DF: You can punt the ball for a first down. (Laughs.) You have to kick it across the line of scrimmage and anyone behind the ball can go get it. They're considered onside like on a kickoff.

DP: Worst thing about the rules in Canadian football.

DF: You lose a down in the last three minutes of a game if you take a delay-of-game penalty.

people wrong.

DP: Do you look at a reporter and wonder if he ever played a sport growing up?

DF: I have more respect if a guy has at least been on the field and competed. If he's gone out there and given everything he had and come up short.

DP: So if you see a talking hairdo or a slob with mustard stains on his shirt, do you think, "How could he possibly know what I go through?"

DF: Sometimes you feel that.

DP: What is the best thing about this year for you?

DF: I do love proving people wrong. People who thought it was a joke that the Bills signed me, especially locally. But more than anything else, I enjoyed going on the field and competing.

DP: Have you kept a scrapbook in your mind of people who have written or said things about you?

DF: Coming out of school, there was a writer in Chicago. **The quote about me being a midget quarterback from a midget school and I'll never amount to anything.** (Both laugh a bit.)

DP: What was...

DF: ...That's after winning **the Heisman,** right? Where does that come from? Does this guy go home and beat his dog afterwards? Where does that type of stuff come from? (Laughs ruefully.)

DP: How did you change during your time away from the NFL?

DF: I enjoyed playing football more.

DP: You fell back in love with it?

DF: I played the game with a smile on my face again. I was able to go on the field and think for myself and make my own decisions. Call my own plays. Be around guys that enjoyed the game. When I was in the NFL the last time around, a lot of that was lost.

DP: How did the league change?

DF: Defenses are more sophisticated, the coverages. Things like that. There's a lot more stuff to learn. People became more open-minded. And the mobile quarterback is now viewed as an asset. Before it was a negative. Until **Joe Montana** and **Steve Young** started doing the things they were doing and **Randall Cunningham,** the first time around with Randall, people viewed that kind of play as a negative but they changed people's thinking. And now you have guys like Jake Plummer, me. Guys that are athletes at the position, running around and making things happen.

DP: Can you name all the CFL teams?

DF: Do you want me to?

DP: Yes. The Montreal Alouettes are out of the league, right?

DF: The Hamilton Tiger Cats. They call them the Ti-cats. Toronto Argonauts. Montreal Alouettes. The Ottawa Roughriders are no longer. The Saskatchewan Rough Riders still stand. The Winnipeg Blue Bombers. The Calgary Stampeders and the British Columbia Lions.

DP: What was the thing with the Rough Riders? Aren't there enough nicknames to go around?

DF: There were eight teams and two of them were named Rough Riders. Twenty-five percent of the league. (Laughs.) What happened was that, way back when, one team was called the Rough Riders. I think it was Saskatchewan. And they disbanded and during that time Ottawa got a franchise and they wanted to be named Rough Riders. So they took the name and I think they were the one-word Roughriders. A little bit different. Then Saskatchewan comes back and they don't care about Ottawa and they take their name back.

DP: Does a day go by that you don't hear a question about the **Hail Mary?**

DF: Someone does bring it up usually. It comes up in a reference or something.

DP: What form does it take?

DF: The first thing is they say, "Oh, I saw that pass against...Notre Dame. Or whoever it was." (Laughs.) What's happening now is that it is coming up less and less because of my success. Now, they say, "You're having a great year. Congratulations on the Pro Bowl." Or whatever.

DP: Dan Marino is 6'5" but when he gets a pass batted down it's never because...

DF: ...he's too short.

DP: Yeah. **It's a great play by the defense.** But every time you throw a pass...

DF: You know it's in people's minds.

DP: You could have a pass batted down by a lineman who is 4'4" and it would be because you are too short. It doesn't make a difference, does it?

DF: It doesn't seem to. That is something that has always bothered me. If you want to knock passes down, and teams have done this to me, Jacksonville and someone else. They did not rush. They figure, "We aren't going to sack the guy anyway. So stay on the line of scrimmage and try to bat down balls." And they batted three or four balls down in the game. **I'll take three or four batted balls as opposed to a pass rush any day of the week.**

DP: Here's some free association. **Elway.**

DF: Last year's Super Bowl and finally getting his due.

DP: **Marino.**

DF: Consistency.

DP: Steve Young.

DF: I always think of Steve in a parallel career to me. Because he started out in Tampa Bay and people doubted him because he was on a bad football team. But then he goes to San Francisco and people think he's God. But he always had the ability and the skills. I have thought we had similar careers.

DP: Bruce Smith.

DF: A legend. The one affiliation I have with Bruce is that when they drafted him they were thinking of drafting me.

DP: You know **I covered your press conference at Trump Tower.**

DF: That was a zoo.

DP: You had the waterfall on the wall there. It was so tacky. I used to have to go to New Jersey Generals games. That was bad. Don't make me do that again.

DF: That was for the people who couldn't get Jets or Giants tickets.

DP: But there was some talent in the USFL.

DF: Fourteen or fifteen guys went to the NFL Pro Bowl the next year.

DP: Is the Heisman trophy overrated?
Does it always go to the right person?

DF: No, it doesn't always go to the right person because it's impossible to select the best player in college football. But I think it has a great tradition so we should not do away with it. We have to back off all the hype. By the end of the year, we have talked about Heisman "candidates." **There is no such thing as a Heisman "candidate."** Right? (Both laugh.) Every person that plays college football is a Heisman candidate. You know? The media does this every year. **Heisman hopeful? Maybe.**

DP: Your favorite short joke. You must hear them all the time.

DF: Whenever we watch football, whatever level, when we see a pass batted down, the first thing out of our mouths is **"He's too short."** (Laughs.) Peyton Manning or whoever. I remember being on the sidelines this year in Indianapolis and Peyton had a few knocked down. It just comes out of my mouth. I don't mean anything by it. My wife started that.

DP: Give me three guys in the NFL that are worth the price of admission, now that you have seen them in person.

DF: Marshall Faulk.

Who else did I see
this year? **Randy Moss,**
but I didn't play
against him. Come on!

DP: Any defenders?

DF: Terrell Buckley always
plays well against us.
And **Aaron Glenn** of
the Jets had a great
game against us in
the Meadowlands.
Keyshawn Johnson is
scary. You feel like you
can't cover him.

DP: Did you want to wear 22 again?

DF: I really wanted it but they have rules
about that stuff in this league.

DP: But John Hadl wore 21?

DF: I know. I told them to list me as a
running back. (Laughs.) But we looked
into it and I had signed my contract as a
quarterback.

DP: Really?

**DF: It says on my contract
"quarterback."**

**DP: Have you had better ideas
than Flutie Flakes?**

DF: I wonder about it when I have to sign 100,000
boxes. (Laughs.) But that was kind of a diamond in
the rough. It was just an idea that we did to try to
help the foundation and it just took off. A lot of
that had to do with my success on the field.

DP: Are there nutritional benefits if my kids eat
Flutie Flakes?

DF: Well, they have no fat and no cholesterol. But a lot
of sugar.

DP: Great. They'll be bouncing off the walls.

DF: Just for a little while. (Laughs.)

DAN PATRICK **SHANNON SHARPE**

If he had a gun, he would

If there is anybody made for this column, it's Shannon Sharpe. He just screamed "Outtakes" to me. This is a guy who practices interviews on his own. He's waiting for the questions. But that doesn't mean there isn't any spontaneity to him. It's just that he has thought about things and he wants to give you a good interview. Maybe he's making up for that other member of the Sharpe family who doesn't talk to the media.

Speaking of Sterling, I was interviewing Shannon with Sterling after the Broncos won their first Super Bowl in 1998. I was really touched at seeing their relationship at such a momentous time. The bond between them is incredible. I think Shannon was happier because he had done something that Sterling could be proud of rather than for any personal reason. His brother was his role model, and he gave something back to his brother in the best possible way: winning a Super Bowl, the mark of supremacy in the field they both competed in. And when Shannon gave Sterling his Super Bowl ring, it was one brother letting another one share in his achievement, a way of saying, "You didn't quite make it all the way and you should have. So let me give you this reward."

So whenever Shannon makes one of his outrageous little statements, I smile — and remember a quiet gesture of his that spoke volumes.

DP: What is the difference between losing to the Giants this week and losing to the Jaguars at home in the 1997 playoffs?

SS: There is still no comparison. The Jacksonville loss was the worst moment, in sports, that I have ever been involved in. Nothing can ever, ever compare to that. (Pause.) **If I had a thousand tongues, Dan, I could not tell you how bad I felt.**

DP: You could never replace that. Even the Super Bowl...

SS: Losing that game hurt worse than winning the Super Bowl felt good.

have shot me.

DP: Wow. But we can't give you a thousand tongues. You talk enough.

DP: How can a guy like **Mike Shanahan** be so intimidating?

SS: Now this is where I can get into trouble. (Laughs.) Maybe it's his glare. We've always been told that people who don't say a lot, those are the ones you need to be afraid of. People aren't afraid of me because I talk all the time. Michael doesn't say a whole lot. He just gives you that look. And you're like, "Now, what is he going to do? Is he going to bench me? Is he going to cut me?"

DP: Did you really used to practice interviewing yourself?

SS: **Before I went to bed, I would talk to myself for twenty minutes in the mirror.** And I'd ask myself an array of questions and most of them were sports-related because I wanted to be involved in sports. So I would say, "OK, Shannon, we won the game and you had this many yards." Or, "Shannon, you dropped the game-winning touchdown. You didn't play so well. What happened?" I was asking myself tough questions because anybody can handle the easy ones.

DP: Can losing make you cry?

SS: The Jacksonville loss was probably the closest I have been to crying since... Let me think. I think the only time I have cried in the past twelve or thirteen years is when I knew that my brother would not be able to play in the NFL anymore.

DP: Because this is your idol who can't play anymore.

SS: Right. I cried. I wanted to know why him and not me. Because I would have gladly, without any hesitation, switched places with him.

DP: Who would win a flex-off, you or **Schwarzenegger?**

SS: Probably me. Because I could hold a pose for thirty seconds and with his heart condition he could hold a pose for two seconds.

DP: But Arnold in his heyday?

SS: **Yeah, but he's no longer in his heyday and I still am.**

DP: What is one thing that you can say on the football field that will really get under a guy's skin?

SS: When you question his ability. Because when you get to this level, everybody thinks he can play. Now, everybody knows they can't be a Pro Bowl player but when you question a guy's ability, like, "I can't believe your play."

DP: Last conversation when you knew you got into somebody's head.

SS: Christian Peter. I will not even tell you what I said. But trust me. I knew he was upset because he turned three to four different shades of red. And his eyes began to water. If he had a gun, he probably would have shot me. (Laughs.)

DP: Who is the last guy to tell you to shut up?

SS: Well, my teammates tell me that every day, so probably someone on my team.

DP: What is John Elway's worst habit?

SS: I don't know if he has one. He stopped dipping. Probably **drinking coffee.**

DP: That's his vice?

SS: Yeah. He drinks about five cups in a two-hour period

DP: That's why he plays so well in the two-minute drill.

SS: That might have something to do with it.

DP: Does **trash talking** run in your family?

SS: Yes. **It started with my grandmother.**

DP: Give me an idea of what your Grandmother Mary would say trash talking.

SS: **Fishing. She had to beat you.** We would always go to this one place and my grandmother had a favorite spot. Every time she would go to that spot, she would catch five or six. One day I beat her to that spot and caught the fish before she got there. She was so upset she told me, "Don't ever, ever go to that spot again." **Hey, it's a free lake. I beat you there!** But she was always, "I caught the most fish. I caught the biggest fish. I'm the better fisherman."

DP: Give me three guys that scare you in the NFL.

SS: There's really no one I keep my distance from but someone I would not like to meet in a dark alley is John Randle. I'm not sure he's all there. (Laughs.)

DP: Two others?

SS: (Pauses.) Obviously Derrick Thomas, because after what he did on national television in front of millions of people, there's no telling what he'd do in a dark alley. And Wayne Simmons, because I have said some things to him that if he had something to hurt me with on the field, he would have.

DP: Should there be special rules for quarterbacks, to protect them?

SS: For my quarterback, yes. **For John, yes. For everybody else, no.**

DP: What is the story you will tell your grandchildren about John Elway?

SS: I'll say that I played with one of the greatest quarterbacks of all time and that **he is a better person than he'll ever be a quarterback.** When I got here, he was already "John Elway." MVP, been to three Super Bowls. And never, ever did he make me feel that he was superior and I was inferior. He talked to me from day one. If I ran the wrong route and he threw an interception, he never showed me up in public.

DP: Why is your locker near the trainer's room?

SS: That's just where they put me. But the way it's positioned, I can see the entire locker room. That's the way I need to be because I need to be able to make fun of someone at any given moment. So I need to see them. **Jokes don't wait around.**

DP: What about seeing who goes in the training room and who's being soft?

SS: Oh, yeah. And I let him know. If a guy is in there too long, I let him know he should go see the cardiologist.

DP: You are well-known for playing through injury. Is that the ultimate test?

SS: No. Playing in pain doesn't do anything.

Can you play in pain and do your normal job?

That's when you are doing something.

DP: Last concert you went to?

SS: Oh, man. Run DMC, 1982.

DP: 1982? You have to get out more.

DP: Where is your Super Bowl ring?

SS: My brother has it. He wears it every Sunday. I think he wears it every day.

DP: We thought that was cubic zirconium.

SS: He has the real thing. I wore it the day I got it. And to a party that day at Mr. Bowlen's house. I've never had it on since.

DP: What's it like in the huddle with Elway?

SS: It depends on the situation. At the start of a game, he talks very fast. But we have been over and over these plays so we know what he is saying. But at the end of a game, if we're behind, he talks so slow it's almost like his speech is slurred. **You can hear-every-word-that-is-said.**

DP: What is your thought on the Minnesota receivers?

SS: Chris Carter has the best pair of hands in the NFL. I'm jealous of that. I'm jealous of Randy Moss's speed. What they have accomplished, I think is fantastic. I'd pay to see them. And there are not a lot of guys I'd pay to see in the NFL.

DP: Top three hands in the NFL.

SS: There is no top three. **There is Cris Carter and then there's everyone else.** No one is even close. He makes more tough catches in a season than guys make in a ten-year career.

DP: Three worst uniforms in the NFL.

SS: For the right price, I could wear anything. (Laughs.) Bengals. Something about the Tiger look. I don't know. The Colts. The all white doesn't do it for me. The Eagles. The all green looks like a leprechaun. And the white and green is like St. Patrick's Day. (Laughs.)

DP: What is the difference between good and great in the NFL?

SS: Barry Sanders impresses me because he does 1,000 yards every year. John has impressed me because he has probably passed for 3,000 yards twelve or thirteen times in his 16-year career. Jerry Rice, 1,000 yards every year but the one he was hurt and his rookie year. That impresses me.

DP: So you're not ready to label Randy Moss great?

SS: No. No. No. I'm sure there have been a lot of guys that came in and tore the league up. Ickey Woods did it. **Did Ickey or did he not?**

DP: He did.

SS: Thank you.

Right before a sack,

I was actually scared when I talked to John Randle. I didn't know if he had prepared for me like he does for a quarterback—load up with information that he would unload on me when I least expected it; read my bio and give me grief.

I got lucky, though. He never let me have it. I came away less scared of Randle than convinced that there's a side to him I had not seen before. That he might be a bit goofy. Maybe even crazy. With a real sense of humor. He has a real fun side to him, so I tried to tap into that and find out what makes him tick. I wanted to find out if the way he behaves on a football field is an act or a reflection of who he really is. And I think that you see the real John Randle out there on Sunday. He has stopped painting his face, but he is still at war.

I also found out later that he is a friend of Warren Sapp, which removed any doubts I may have had about whether or not he's crazy. So John Randle is a little crazy—but in a good way.

DP: Is it possible for a grown man to look good in the color purple?

JR: Yes it is. Look at **Barney.**

DP: Is Barney a grown man?

JR: I think he is. (Both laugh.)

DP: I know you're a wrestling fan. "Stone Cold" Steve Austin? Why?

JR: Because he is the toughest SOB in the world. That's what he says. I believe him.

DP: So he's tougher than you?

JR: We're probably the same level. He's from Texas. I'm from Texas. So we people from Texas think of ourselves or anybody from Texas as being the best.

everything is silent.

DP: You would like a piece of him, wouldn't you?

JR: A piece of "Stone Cold"? That's a tough question because he's from Texas. I'd like to be his tag-team partner, though.

DP: I see. **If you and he were a tag team, who would you like to go against?**

JR: (No hesitation.) Kevin Greene and Kevin Gogan.

DP: Give me the three dirtiest players in the league?

JR: Steve Wisniewski of the Raiders. Frank Winters of the Packers. And Kevin Gogan.

DP: What does it take to be a dirty player?

JR: Dirty means the unnecessary stuff that they do. The holding when it's too blatant. I mean, some holding is understandable. And some other stuff is understandable. It's when they take it to another level.

DP: So what does Gogan do?

JR: They all have different things. Gogan, because he's taller than you, tries to punch down on you. Punch down on my helmet and stuff. Tries to slow me down just by punching on me.

DP: Wisniewski?

JR: **He tries to grab you and step on the back of your leg. He's like a bully.**

DP: Winters?

JR: I think he thinks he's Superman. Running downfield after plays, diving at guys. Over the pile.

DP: How do you get back at them?

JR: **Keep coming. Go at the same speed every play. Never give up.**

DP: Do you go through the media guide and pick up stuff specifically to use on guys?

JR: Sometimes I do.

DP: For instance? Who was a guy that you found something juicy on and couldn't wait to get on the field and use it?

JR: **Aaron Taylor** when he was on Green Bay. He had just bought a Yukon and he had a 1968 Impala convertible car. (Both laugh.) And he loved his Impala and he loved his new Yukon. So I started asking him if I could use them.

DP: You probably can't talk enough to a rookie quarterback.

JR: You're gonna throw everything but the kitchen sink at that guy.

DP: So you're singing to Charlie Batch every day?

JR: **I'm singing. I'm talking. Trying anything. Be his best friend. Be his pen pal if I could.**

DP: Do you speak a different language?

JR: I know a little French. A little bit of Spanish. The other languages, I kind of fake it. (Both chuckle.)

DP: You don't strike me as someone who would be quoting French during a football game.

JR: **You'd be surprised what you can pick up at the end of a movie.**

DP: Do you use movies as motivation or as quotes to use during a game?

JR: Both ways.

DP: For instance.

JR: *Road Warrior.*

DP: OK. *Mad Max.* As motivation but will you use lines from that?

JR: Oh, yeah. **"Lord Humongous, Ruler of the Wasteland."** Awesome, man. He was the man! I couldn't understand how that guy got so buffed. There were no weights around. You ever see that movie?

DP: John. That movie is not true.

JR: I know that. But when you watch a movie you just wonder about certain things. Why is this going on? How is this guy so buffed and big?

DP: Give me some **physiques that don't belong in the NFL.**

JR: Physiques? Now, I'm from a small town in Texas. Physiques?

DP: Bodies.

JR: <u>Gilbert Brown</u> is one of them. (Pause.) Kevin Gogan. (Laughs.)

DP: Gilbert Brown. That physique. What does it make you think of?

JR: **It's like, when the season is over, some guys rest. And some guys rest a whole lot more.**

DP: What is your **pre-game ritual?** Does it vary with the opponent?

JR: It probably varies. Same meal pre-game. Not take a shower the night before. No shower morning of. Probably don't brush my teeth. (Laughs.) Probably take a picture of the guy and put it in my sock. **Listen to some Frank Sinatra** before the game. If not Frank, I'd throw in some Jim Morrison. Stuff like that.

DP: There's a big difference between Sinatra and Jim Morrison.

JR: If it's a really intense game and I have to be focused, I throw in Jim. Break on through to the other side. Break on through. Gotta have that.

DP: What is your favorite moment during a sack?

JR: Right before you get it. It seems like you stop breathing. Everything is so silent. It seems like it takes an hour to get there and it's really a split second. **It's so quiet and it's just a wonderful feeling.**

DP: Have you ever felt sorry for a quarterback?

JR: No.

DP: Never?

JR: Never.

DP: Even after you've hit him and he doesn't get up? And you've heard the wind go out of him?

JR: Nope.

DP: Never.

JR: Never. **I never feel sorry for a quarterback. I've been mad at a quarterback for not giving me a sack.**

DP: Toughest guys to sack.

JR: **Brett Favre. Steve Young. Warren Moon.**

DP: What is it about those three?

JR: They just won't go down. They try to stay up.

DP: Favre is strong, Young is elusive and Moon...

JR: **Warren Moon is sneaky. He has eyes in the back of his head.** He will wait until that last second when you are right up on him and he will just duck. And he'll just walk back to the huddle real casual. He'll smile like, "Yeah, you missed."

DP: Is it a compliment to be **double- or triple-teamed?**

JR: Yes it is.

DP: Do you view it that way during a game?

JR: No, it's more of a decoy. I'm a decoy.

DP: It frustrates you.

JR: I get louder and more psyched out. When they are double- or triple-teaming me, it allows my teammates to get to the quarterback.

DP: How long have you been painting your face?

JR: About five years. It was before the first game and the whole defensive line was doing it. Everybody had different ways of doing it. Some guys got bored but I kept doing it.

DP: And no one else does it?

JR: No. A few guys have tried on other teams. But I'm the only one on the Vikings doing it.

DP: What's the most surprising thing you have learned about **Randy Moss?**

JR: **That he is a very competitive person. And he tries so hard to do everything correctly.**

DP: What is your favorite rookie hazing story?

JR: Quadry Ismail. "The Missile." **We tied him to a chair and took him outside underneath the goalpost. It was about ten degrees outside and snowing. He was wearing nothing but his jock.** (Laughs.)

DP: That's cruel.

JR: That's part of being a rookie.

DP: Favorite **Tony Dungy** story.

JR: It's not really a story. More of how he gets his point across. So subtle. He doesn't say that much. **He could just throw a film on and say, "Here is a guy making some great plays for us." And the film will be the guy not making great plays. That's Tony.**

DP: Would you rather intercept a pass and return it for a touchdown or hit a guy so hard he whimpers?

JR: Hit somebody so hard that they whimper.

DP: Why?

JR: **That's just my mentality.**

DP: Free association. Pickup trucks.

JR: Love 'em.

DP: **"Columbo."**

JR: Love that show.

DP: Why?

JR: Because he's so unorthodox. **He's like me. He doesn't really fit in and people think he's a nuisance. But he still gets the job done.**

DP: Al Pacino.

JR: A tough man. With a lot of bullets in him.

DP: The chase or the sack itself.

JR: **The chase.**

DP: If you know players are using steroids, do you lose respect for them?

JR: Yes.

DP: Do you have to keep quiet? The code of the NFL?

JR: **Most guys don't let me know because they know how I feel about it.**

DP: What's the worst thing someone could say about you as a football player?

JR: That I didn't give my all. Or wasn't dedicated to the game.

DP: **Do you truly love the game?**

JR: Yes I do. As I see it, I'm not supposed to be here. I was only supposed to be here for a week or two, back in training camp in 1990. And I'm still here.

DAN PATRICK   MIKE PIAZZA

You gotta squat at

(I) played golf a few years ago at La Costa in Carlsbad, CA, with Mike Piazza in a foursome with Mark McGwire and Eric Karros. I had a great time with Piazza. It was like my older brother Bill was sitting in the cart with me. And you don't want to sit with my brother Bill for too long because he is a very sick individual.

Piazza just sees the world differently. He has his own words and expression for things (as you'll see). As often happens with athletes, we talked about everything but sports: music, stereo equipment, fashion. We were oblivious to what we were supposed to be doing. We played terribly. McGwire and Karros trounced us. Piazza unhooked McGwire's golf bag so when he pulled away in the cart, the bag flew off. McGwire was sure I did it and was mad at me all day. He kept assuring me he'd get me. Piazza kept putting carrots in my drink and he put a frog in my golf bag.

I'm sure there's a serious side to young Mike but I have yet to find it. Which is fine.

DP: Do you ever get tired of squatting?

MP: (Laughs a bit.) Actually, yeah I do. Sure.

DP: Because Pudge Rodriguez has told me that when he is out at the mall walking around, to relax, he'll just squat.

MP: Oh, yeah. During all the team meetings, when they are talking about signs on the field, you gotta squat. Or at a party or standing around at a bar.

DP: At a party?

MP: I'll bend down that way.

DP: You'll just squat.

MP: You get a good lay of the land that way.

parties.

DP: Is catcher the worst position to play in baseball?

MP: Worst as in most work? Or most pain? Or what?

DP: All of the above, isn't it?

MP: Yeah. Definitely.

DP: On a day in August in St. Louis and you're putting on the pads, that's not fun, is it?

MP: It's not fun. But if you need to lose some weight, **it beats Jenny Craig, I guess.**

DP: Compare the fans in L.A., New York and Florida.

MP: (Laughs.) All of them have two arms and two legs. They wear hats and things like that. (Laughs.)

DP: Are they good? Don't get serious on me. This isn't an essay test.

MP: Are they vocal?

DP: This isn't the SAT test. But you'd be Prop 48, I think.

MP: That's true. I think L.A. fans are extremely supportive. They come out in numbers but they aren't as vocal as East Coast fans. Maybe because they are farther away in the stands. I don't know. It's a different atmosphere in L.A. **Organ music and lazy evenings.**

DP: Give me the three best heavy metal bands of all time.

MP: What kind of metal? Speed metal? Glam metal? Like gothic metal? Death metal?

DP: Just your three favorite bands of all time.

MP: My favorite speed metal band is **Slayer.** My favorite glam metal band is **Motley Crüe.** My favorite just-straight metal band would be **AC/DC.**

DP: The thing that I've never understood is why is it when the pitcher gives up a home run, the next guy gets hit?

MP: That's true. (Laughs.) It's a thing of being in the wrong place at the wrong time. Bad timing.

DP: Don't you feel bad if you hit a tater and the guy on deck gets plunked? Because you hit a home run.

MP: Better him than me.

DP: That's why you want to hit third.

MP: Or hit behind John Olerud.

DP: Give me one-word answers to describe these swings. Griffey.

MP: Fluid.

DP: Gwynn.

MP: Improvisation.

DP: McGwire.

MP: Powerful is obvious, I guess. (Pauses.)

DP: I got a better idea. If you were going to attach a rock band to these swings, or a band. So Tony Gwynn.

MP: (Laughing hard.) The Temptations.

DP: Mark McGwire.

MP: Man of War.

DP: Griffey.

MP: Steve Miller Band. "Fly Like an Eagle."

DP: Very good.

MP: (Sings.) Doo-doo-doot-doot.

DP: Bonds.

MP: Tupac.

DP: What about your swing?

MP: My swing. It's unorthodox. I'd have to go with Dream Theater.

DP: (A bit puzzled.) Dream Theater? I was thinking of Yanni.

DP: Give me three tough pitchers to handle.

MP: Turk Wendell is pretty tough.

DP: Why?

MP: He just has a lot of movement on the ball. Everything is moving out of his hand. And he really doesn't know where it's going.

DP: Who else?

MP: **Ramon Martinez was tough.** Movement again. **He used to ruin my gloves, shred my leather.** (Laughs.)

DP: And?

MP: I want to say this. Remember last year in the All Star game with Javy Lopez and Ugueth Urbina? He struggled, man. That guy looks tough to catch, dude. I was glad I was out of the game.

DP: Really.

MP: I thought, "This guys looks filthy."

DP: What is the best thing you ever learned from Tommy Lasorda?

MP: How to get a free meal. (Laughs.)

DP: And Tommy has had a lot of free meals.

MP: Tommy has never paid ... **Tommy has his meal money in a mutual fund before the road trip, dude.**

DP: Give me three actresses that you could call up right now that would impress me.

MP: I'll tell you what, dude, my Rolodex is sorry right now. I don't go with the actress. I go with sort of a lower, Victoria's Secret sort of lineup. I don't go for the big names. They're too much trouble.

DP: High maintenance?

MP: Too much. **I can't afford the Mariah Careys. That's just too high profile.**

DP: So you're no Derek Jeter? You're no Puff Daddy?

MP: No. I'm no Derek Jeter. He can have Mariah Carey. I'll stay with page seven of the Victoria's Secret catalog. Some girl from Brazil. You look at her and say, "That girl is hot." And then turn the page.

DP: What is the catcher's best friend?

MP: Definitely his cup. That's a given.

DP: Do people try to steal them or hide them on you?

MP: No. Luckily there is a steady supply. You always have backup.

DP: Mark McGwire told me that last year in Houston someone stole his cup. It bummed him out because he'd had it his whole career.

MP: Are you serious?

DP: Somebody stole it.

MP: I usually end up cracking a few each year. You guys had me all over ESPN. I had my nuts split and **you're showing me screaming in agony.**

DP: Best football team cheerleaders.

MP: Without a doubt, the Raiderettes, man. There might be a distant second out there somewhere but I'm not aware of them.

I've seen them all. I've scouted 'em.

DP: Tell me the three best catchers of all time.

MP: Bill Dickey. Johnny Bench. Roy Campanella.

DP: So you look at them more as catchers than as hitters.

MP: Absolutely. Catching is a defensive position. It's got to be. I'd like to consider myself a catcher who's a good hitter.

DP: As opposed to...

MP: A hitter who catches.

DP: You've probably been unfairly criticized that way.

MP: That's something I have to live with...But I don't really accept it. But I just try to keep doing what I am doing. You can't change what people think. You might try to influence them.

DP: I didn't like the way the whole Dodger thing played out because I...

MP: **Dude, that was a nightmare. That was a joke.** It was a big setup from the start. The reporter knew I was going for my extension. The guy had no credibility because he wasn't with the team for like eight months. Now, all of a sudden he's an authority on my leadership abilities? This reporter is like, "Piazza is going for a hundred million." And it was a setup. **A joke.**

DP: What went through your mind when Kevin Brown got $105 million from the Dodgers?

MP: Well, I wouldn't lie and say that it wasn't disappointing. Because of the fact that they were so adamant about drawing a line in the sand with me. I felt vindicated as a player, though, knowing it wasn't a financial issue. **It was personal.** So, that's fine. If you don't think I'm worth it, I can't force you to pay me. And they wouldn't even give me a chance. That's how much they wanted me. They didn't say, "Take this much money or we'll trade you." **They just traded me.**

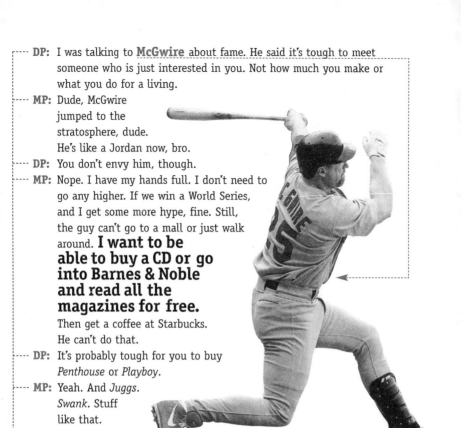

DP: I was talking to **McGwire** about fame. He said it's tough to meet someone who is just interested in you. Not how much you make or what you do for a living.

MP: Dude, McGwire jumped to the stratosphere, dude. He's like a Jordan now, bro.

DP: You don't envy him, though.

MP: Nope. I have my hands full. I don't need to go any higher. If we win a World Series, and I get some more hype, fine. Still, the guy can't go to a mall or just walk around. **I want to be able to buy a CD or go into Barnes & Noble and read all the magazines for free.** Then get a coffee at Starbucks. He can't do that.

DP: It's probably tough for you to buy *Penthouse* or *Playboy*.

MP: Yeah. And *Juggs*. *Swank*. Stuff like that.

DP: So what, do you have somebody pick it up for you?

MP: No. I go to the sleazy joint on the corner.

DP: And they don't recognize you?

MP: No, it's some guy from Bangladesh. (Laughs.)

DP: What is the craziest thing a woman has done to meet you?

MP: Like follow you home?

DP: Yeah. At the hotel. Or disguised as room service.

MP: I have had some follow me home. I'm driving 90 mph and changing lanes. You also get off the bus at three in the morning in Cincinnati and there's like a couple of girls there. It's weird, dude.

DP: Because you're a one-woman man.

MP: Let me say this. In this day and age, you have to be careful, and I don't want to sound weird or nothing, but I at least like to screen the person a little bit. **There are all kinds of potential problems.**

So somebody's got my cup.

(T) here was a time not so long ago when Mark McGwire looked like he might be done. He was battling injuries and missing a lot of games. In 1993 and '94 he had a total of 18 home runs. In August of '94, I went out to Cleveland to do a "Sunday Conversation" with him. We were booked for a half hour, but Mark being Mark, we talked for an hour. Later that day, we ended up at the same place for lunch and Mark covered my tab. But, Mark being Mark, he had the waitress come over and say that the restaurant manager paid it.

In 1999, Mark and I filmed the "Sweet 62" *SportsCenter* commercial. He loved the idea of mocking the system that turns baseballs into million-dollar investment pieces. The agency had written lines for him, but he used his own words in the ad. He mentioned that he appreciated that I wanted to talk to him back when a lot of people thought he was on the decline. He said, "You were there at a tough time." He hugged me — for real.

That's Mark McGwire to me. There is no facade with him. He's the same guy he always was. But his failures have made him successful. He has learned from them and is very open about sharing what he has learned. Sometimes he may even reveal too much of himself, but he can't help it. He's honest.

As for his post-70 homeruns life, I don't know if he's enjoyed it. I don't know if we have allowed him to. In this day and age, we tend to smother an athlete and an event. We keep asking McGwire how he feels without letting him come up for air so he can find out for himself.

DP: Name some pitchers that you would consider friends.

MM: Roger Clemens. Randy Johnson. Robb Nen. Those three are pretty good friends.

DP: What would a typical conversation be?

MM: The times I have been around those guys we have just talked baseball in general. About what has been happening recently or some moves that have been made. I have never talked about times I faced them.

DP: (Laughs.)

MM: All three of them get me out more than I get hits. (Laughs.)

DP: The thing is, though, you could go 0 for 10 against any one of them, with 10 strikeouts, and then hit a 450-foot homer.

MM: Right.

DP: And it crushes them because they know that's all people talk about. It's like Randy Johnson. I don't know what your batting average is against him but it is probably not too good.

MM: Yeah.

DP: **But you hit one of the longest home runs ever off him.** And that's what people, I'm sure, bring up to him.

MM: Yeah, I bet they do. But in the back of my mind I know that he gets me out a lot more than just that one hit.

DP: I know that guys will say they are not in fear at the plate. You are not afraid of a pitcher. But are you afraid of failure when you go to the plate?

MM: Maybe when I was younger I was. Today? No. Not the way I am mentally at the plate now. I am my own hitting coach now. **I know my swing like the back of my hand.** I make adjustments pitch to pitch, at-bat to at-bat.

DP: Do pitchers ask for your autograph during the season?

MM: Oh, sure.

DP: Guys who served up home runs to you?

MM: Yeah. I'm sure they have. Guys are pretty good about it. They usually ask me personally. And I usually sign on the last day of a home stand. And the same thing on the road.

DP: Did Greg Maddux ask for an autograph?

MM: I just signed some autographs for him. It was a pretty cool photo of him pitching against me.

DP: What happened on that at-bat?

MM: I don't know.

DP: (Laughs.) Maybe that's why he wanted that one signed. He can tell people, "Here I am striking him out." (Both laugh.)

MM: Well, he has done that!

DP: Are you tired of you?

MM: (Laughs.) **The thing I am most tired of is** if I don't do something or if I don't play in a game, they always seem to mention my name anyway. And I think, "You know, there's a newspaper there, and people can read the box score the next day to see what I did or if I didn't play."

DP: You know there are teams right now that have no chance of winning. The Oakland A's are not going to win the World Series. The Kansas City Royals. The Minnesota Twins. Is that bad for baseball?

MM: That's not good but it's been like that for baseball for a long time. Now it is just emphasized because of the big salaries. And there's only half a dozen teams that can afford top-notch players.

DP: But isn't it the haves and the have nots?

MM: It is and that's a tough thing. That's why I think if you don't think there are going to be problems in 2001, then you are not on this earth. You're in outer space somewhere. I think everybody is concerned about it. You have to be concerned about it.

DP: It scares me as a baseball fan.

MM: It should.

DP: What is your favorite **Jose Canseco** story?

MM: I think the time when he got caught speeding

down in Florida and he was using **rocket fuel in his car.**
That was hilarious.

DP: (Laughing.)

MM: You know? Rocket fuel?

DP: And we're not talking about Clemens here. Were you disappointed that Madonna chose Jose instead of you?

MM: She probably didn't know who the hell I was! (Laughing.) **But if she wants to give me a call now, that would be all right.**

DP: Give me the craziest story you have of a woman throwing herself at you this past year.

MM: I haven't had any.

DP: Stop it!

MM: (Laughs.) I haven't had anything that's... off the top of my head that was crazy. In dealing with a woman.

DP: You are playing Pebble Beach and you are on the eighth hole overlooking the water. Your second shot and you have to carry the ocean. Or Randy Johnson, 3-2 count, bases loaded. Pick your poison.

MM: **I'd take Randy Johnson.**

DP: You like your chances of doing something with Randy Johnson?

MM: I'll take my chances with Randy. (Laughs.)

DP: Is it because you look down at a **golf ball**

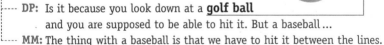

and you are supposed to be able to hit it. But a baseball...

MM: The thing with a baseball is that we have to hit it between the lines. There is a greater opening than trying to hit a ball into a cup. We don't have to deal with trees. We don't have to deal with sand traps. We don't have to deal with water. I like my chances better playing baseball.

DP: So, you kissed Helen Hunt. And you kissed the Pope's ring.

MM: What else can a man ask for?

DP: If you could do one of them again, and God is listening to your answer, which one would it be? Helen Hunt's lips or the Pope's ring?

MM: I'd take both.

DP: Oh, stop it! You can't. You get one.

MM: I get one. I'd definitely do the Pope again. Yeah. I'd like to spend more time with him.

DP: (Laughs.) So Helen Hunt gets blown off, just like that?

MM: I think Helen Hunt would take the Pope over me. (Both laugh.)

DP: I know you have thought about this. **You could have an off year and hit 50.**

MM: Yeah but if people think 70 is going to be easy or 60 is going to be easy... (trails off). For 37 years, people tried to break the 61 barrier and all of a sudden it's broken twice. Now they're talking about breaking 60 like it's nothing. They even treat 50 like it's nothing. You know only 18 guys have ever hit 50 home runs in a season. Ever. And only four guys have hit 60. For people to sit back and assume it will happen, it's not realistic. **What happened last year might never happen again.**

DP: Are you **superstitious?**

MM: I shaved off my goatee after the last game in 1992.
We lost to Toronto in the playoffs. I have not shaved it off since.

DP: You sound like you're superstitious.

MM: Well, I'm 35 now. If I shave it off, I look 20.

DP: The better for you to get more women!

MM: (Laughing.) So we're back to the woman situation.

DP: I am trying to help you here.

MM: How are you going to help me?

DP: Just trying to help you find a woman.
We'll start the **1-800-MARK MCGWIRE line.**

MM: Great.

DP: Did anything hurt last year?
Something that was written that
took some fun out of it.

MM: It's obvious.
The androstene stuff.

DP: That's the one thing that you
would say hurt.

MM: I don't think it hurt anything because
they made something out of nothing.
I just think about the way the AP writer
went about it, digging in my locker. And

the way they did their investigative story, calling the IOC and the NFL. It came out like there was something wrong with it. And believe me that stuff has nothing to do with the hand-eye coordination of hitting a baseball. If it did, there would be lot more guys hitting 70 home runs.

DP: Explain to me what happened in Houston. You told me that you gave away everything. But you had one item stolen last year.

MM: My cup, one I had since the minor leagues. And it didn't make it from the Houston locker room to the St. Louis locker room. **So, somebody's got my cup.**

DP: (Laughing.) Did you ever wonder why somebody wanted your protective cup?

MM: I don't know. Hopefully, we won't see it for sale on the Internet.

DP: If we see it on the Home Shopping Network ...

MM: Oh, I'm going to buy it back. Yeah.

DP: The same cup from the minor leagues?

MM: Yeah. It was a good one, too.

DP: Some guys that you would pay to bring your son to see play.

MM: Larry Walker. Roger Clemens. Ken Griffey Jr. **Kirby Puckett,** too.

DP: Is it a goal to hit **700 home runs?**

MM: I don't know. I couldn't say. The first realistic number is 500. For me to reach Hank Aaron's record, I would have to get on a fast horse right now.

DP: Well, if you put together **a few more 70's ....**

MM: (Cackles.) **Okey, dokey!**

DP: That's not just a dream, is it? To hit 700 home runs.

MM: God willing, if I get close enough, yeah, it would be a dream. But right now it's so far in the distance.

DP: OK. We'll get you to 500 and start talking about 600.

MM: Sure.

I think those guys were just

(T) he first time I met Warren Sapp was in January of 1995, when the Super Bowl was in Miami and Sapp was coming out of the University of Miami. Sapp introduced himself to me and said, "I watch you every night and I think that you do a great job." And I replied, "I thought you were the most dominating player in college football." We laughed and agreed that we had a mutual admiration society. I later talked to him on the phone a few times and found that he always gives direct, honest answers.

As time went on, I found myself rooting for him, even when he had his problems on draft day after testing positive for marijuana. It was interesting to watch the most important day of his life sort of flash by. I admit, though, that I was wondering if this was the same guy, and if he was worth a number-one pick. Well, the Buccaneers have reaped the benefits of giving a second chance to a guy that deserved one. If I were starting a defense, I'd take Sapp first, over anybody in the league.

We spoke during the early part of the 1999–2000 NFL season. And despite the frustrations the Bucs have faced, Sapp was his usual, jovial self. But then, we already knew that Warren Sapp knows how to handle adversity.

DP: You play hard every single down. Now, I don't know who taught you that. I mean is that something that's just instilled in you?

WS: My days back in Miami. The first day I walked in they said — if you want to learn how to play, look at that wall. And there's a wall of all the great ones that played before me — **Russell Maryland, Cortez Kennedy, Jerome Brown, Ruben Carter** and all of those guys. They said open up the film and watch it. And that's just how we play the game.

DP: All the trash talking with someone like Brett Favre. Does it work when you talk to somebody and try to get into their head?

happy they had face masks.

WS: I don't think it does when you talk about somebody like Brett Favre. But maybe somebody like Donovan McNabb. Last week when I was jiving with him a little bit. But maybe all of a sudden — when his first receiver's covered, he doesn't look for that 2nd and 3rd receiver. He's thinking — oh my God, where is that rush coming from?

DP: Give me a sense of a conversation you would have with Brett Favre.

WS: It really depends on the situation. Around playoff time, I was asking what did he get for Christmas. And what his wife cooked — stuff like that. (Laughs.)

DP: But what would you say to a rookie? You got to love it when a new quarterback comes in because it's fresh meat.

WS: Oh yeah, I really just felt like — we had a chance to really go after this kid. And I felt like he was a great athlete, but we always look at that as a challenge. As a matter of fact, the first time I told him, **"I'll be right back, rookie. Now, stay right there where you at."** It was just one of those things.

DP: Now, do you get preferential treatment from Tony Dungy, because you're a neighbor of his?

WS: His house was being built and I didn't even know it. They didn't even tell me that his house was being built down the street from me. But once we moved in, then they told me — oh yeah, Tony's moving in down the street. **I went — oh my God, wait till they hear about this at the job. They're going to kill me.**

DP: How do you dance around the question when people ask you about Trent Dilfer, that you want to instill confidence or let him know you're behind him—but then there's also a part of you that says—maybe he's not the guy?

WS: I'm not dancing around the question because I feel like he is the guy. I know his position is the most demanding on the field. But he's done a good job for us. And right now we don't have anybody else. What are we going to do, turn to Shaun King? C'mon.

DP: Not yet.

WS: The future's now. That's what this ball club's looking at. The future's now. We can't say — we're going to groom Shaun King and in three years — in three years I might not be here.

DP: Does Dilfer try to do too much?

WS: In some instances I think so. Just throw the damn ball out of bounds and let's line back up. You know, let's not try to make a heroic play because you're not Fran Tarkenton. Just throw it out of bounds, let us go out and play great defense and we'll give you the ball in a better position.

DP: Can you explain the Tampa Bay uniforms?

WS: These new ones are sweet.

DP: Yeah, but those old ones — the original ones — I mean, you couldn't feel like a man if you put those on, could you?

WS: No, I didn't feel like a man with **Bucco Bruce**

on the side of my head with an earring in his right ear. **But you know, these new ones are just lovely.**

I mean, 'cause we have a combination where we can do — dark bottoms, light tops — dark tops, dark bottoms or vice versa.

DP: Can you imagine Dick Butkus being concerned about the uniform he was wearing? Or Ray Nitschke?

WS: I think those guys were just happy that they had face masks.

DP: Give me guys that played before you that you just say — that's a football player.

WS: Deacon Jones, Joe Greene, Jerome Brown, Howie Long.

DP: But you didn't pick out any offensive guys there.

WS: Nah, because they're not down and dirty. **They just reap the benefits from all of our hard work.**

DP: You get no love, do you?

WS: It's a thankless job.

DP: Give me three offensive linemen that you know when you're up against them you got a full afternoon.

WS: Larry Allen, Randall McDaniel and Jeff Hastings in Detroit.

DP: You know that when you line up that you got your work cut out.

WS: You got to bring your hard hat to the job. Yeah. **And don't forget any of your tools — bring the big toolbox and your hard hat, because it's going to be an all-day affair.**

DP: Raised by your mother — Annie Roberts. What was the most endearing quality that she gave to you or the lesson that she gave to you?

WS: Always be straightforward with somebody. If you don't bullshit nobody, they won't bullshit you. If you shoot it straight, nine times out of ten, you'll get everything that you possibly can to better yourself as a person. Everything else will take care of itself.

DP: Is there a quarterback you haven't sacked yet that you just — you're waiting for and you got something to say to him once you get there?

WS: He's gone now. John Elway suckered me when I was in my second year. I had him by one hand but he slipped it for about a 12-yard gain. I was dying to get that one back. But I'm not going to get a shot at it.

DP: Can we do away with Astroturf?

WS: If we can put a man on the moon, we can grow grass inside.

DP: Give me a **typical meal** for you.

WS: Chicken Caesar Salad to start off. Portobello mushrooms, mozzarella and tomatoes — that's just an appetizer. A nice double portion of lamb chops with some mint jelly — go to work. And a lot of bread. And a lot of water around the table. **A lot of bread** and water, and then after that — key lime pie to finish it off.

DP: I have a Manute Bol autographed jersey, so — when I think of you, I'll think of Manute, because it looks like he could be part of a meal for you.

WS: Get some Manute and mint jelly and I'll eat him up, too.

DP: Free association. **Mean Joe Greene.**

WS: Killer.

DP: **Chris Rock.**

WS: Hilarious.

DP: **Instant replay.**

WS: Awwrrggh.

DP: **Game Day.**

WS: Fun time.

DP: **Bill Clinton.**

WS: (Laughs.) Monica.

DP: How did you come up with the name Mercedes for your daughter?

WS: I thought it was a beautiful name and I figured I was going to have a beautiful little girl, by looking at myself in the mirror.

DP: But do you drive a Mercedes?

WS: Yeah, I have four of them.

DP: Well, why do you need four cars?

WS: Well, I own four of them.

DP: I know, but why four?

WS: Well, one's a truck. So we can all pile in and go camping and get it dirty. And my wife and my baby can get in it and throw Goldfish all over the place. They just destroy my truck. The 600s are for me because I always wanted a coupe and a convertible. And I had to get one for my wife. You know how that is.

DP: Do you have a favorite guy on another team in the league?

WS: Yeah, Johnny Randle. **I love Johnny Randle. I love the way he plays the game.** I love the way he talks trash. And I love the way he just goes out there and has a ball, 'cause that's what it's all about is having fun.

DP: Have you ever given a
pre-game pep talk?

WS: No.

DP: Have you heard one that you had to laugh at?

WS: Yeah, when I first got here in Tampa, we used to get about eight of them a day.

DP: Well, who would give you one that made you laugh?

WS: Sam Wyche.

DP: What did he say?

WS: **The worst.** He'd give you a story about some guys in Seattle that did something while he was in Cincinnati. And you know, you're looking at this like — what does this have to do with anything that we're about to do today? And he was just the silliest guy. He was his own band. One-man band. All by himself.

DP: **So you had to snicker.**

WS: Oh, I laughed all the time. I'd be in the back of the room just covering my face.

I'm even uncomfortable

(P)ete Sampras has been able to maintain a remarkable level of consistency and achievement, yet all we focus on are negatives. People say he doesn't have a personality. I found out otherwise. He's never won the French. So what? I'll live with the 12 Grand Slams. He's the Larry Holmes of tennis. Who did he go against? It's all nitpicking, and it's all unfair.

We talked after he won the Stella Artois tournament in June of 1999. He spent an hour and a half with me and he was by far the most surprising person I've interviewed for the magazine. He mocked himself and he mocked the people who think he doesn't have a personality. And he did it all with a wit and intelligence that was so facile that I find it hard to believe how far off the mark his sleepy reputation is.

Of all the athletes I have interviewed, Pete Sampras reminds me the most of myself. I see that desire to be great but no need to be recognized for it. You play because you want to play. Even if people keep criticizing you for all that you aren't, you just keep playing the way you want to play. Eventually, you'll be recognized.

DP: Is there a difference in your mood after a win as opposed to a loss?

PS: Uh, yeah. When I lose, I'm down and out. Disappointed. But it depends on the loss, it depends on who I lost to, when, what tournament. But today's win was nice. I needed it.

DP: It's funny because I was talking to your agent and I said, "He's going to beat Tim Henman." And this was a few days ago. I didn't know. I don't know who plays in the Stella Artois.

PS: Come on!

DP: It's not big. It's a beer. **Everybody thinks Stella is a woman. It's a beer.** Have you had one?

with my success.

PS: (Laughs.) No. I don't drink beer. But you know what I did do? **I actually bought an ESPN Magazine.**

DP: You did? To see what this was going to be about?

PS: Kind of. I saw your thing with **David Cone.**

DP: And then you got nervous.

PS: He was talking about "Spanktravision." And I was like, "Whoaaaa!" (Laughs.) Jeez.

DP: I like his home run call: "You can grab your ankles!" (Both laugh.)

PS: He's got personality.

DP: There was a lot of stuff we couldn't use, actually.

DP: When would I see your ego?

PS: On the tennis court. That's the only time that my ego comes into play.

DP: But how can I see that?

PS: It's not obvious but deep down, when I lose, my ego is hurt.

DP: I'm just curious. I don't see it.

PS: Well, it's on court.

DP: But you don't talk. You don't throw things. You're not a demonstrative guy on the court.

PS: It comes down to your play. You can do what you want or say what you want but it comes down to what you do when the ball is in play. That's my attitude and personality. I'm very humble. **I'm even uncomfortable with all the success I have had over my career.**

DP: You probably do it to keep yourself hungry. As soon as you think you're great, somebody comes along and knocks your ass down.

PS: That's pretty much the kiss of death.

DP: I have never heard you say that you are the best player in the world. Or that you would like to cut off **Marcelo Rios' ponytail.**

PS: I'd like to say it but I bite my tongue.

DP: Should you judge greatness on what you haven't done?

PS: Not in my sport. You can't compare the time I am playing now with 40 or 50 years ago. So, it's what I have done. That's the true test.

DP: But do people say, "Yeah, but..."

PS: Well, it's not a black and white world, Dan. (Both laugh.) It's not.

DP: I'm going to write this down. Getting a little therapy here.

PS: Sure, critics and historians and old-timers will always say that until I win the French blah blah

blah, I won't be the greatest ever. But, not to take anything away from Rod Laver or that era, it's a different sport now. Laver was pretty much beating guys that he was just better than on any surface. He didn't have the clay court animals that you have today. **He had to worry about a couple of guys. I have to worry about 50 guys.**

DP: But your life is complete without a French Open?

PS: Yeah. My life would be fine. I would be disappointed but I never thought I would win what I have won so far anyway.

DP: What is the best thing about being famous?

PS: You can play the best golf courses in the world. You can get into any restaurant at any time. That's pretty much it.

DP: The worst thing about being famous.

PS: Every time I am at an event, when I get out of my car or leave the locker room, I am recognized. Some mornings I don't want to deal with it. Constantly being stared at. Autographs. Pictures. Rude people.

DP: It hurts to be called boring, doesn't it?

PS: Yeah it does, and **you know it's a bunch of crap.** It is. No one is boring.

DP: I agree.

PS: When I hear stuff like that, I take it personally. Like a personal attack on my character. You're the way you are. I am the way I am. For someone to say he's boring, **it's a cop-out.** Instead of trying to figure out what makes me tick or why I do what I do, the easy thing is to say, "He's boring." And call it a day.

DP: (Laughs.)

PS: It's totally true. That's the way I look at the media sometimes. You hear all of these complaints about the men's game having no personalities or rivalries. It's all negative stuff. Instead of wondering why Andrei Medvedev is in the finals of the French when he is ranked 100th, why not say that the game is so damn strong now that anyone can do anything? There are no sure things. **It's just the negative stuff and I'm tired of it.**

DP: Barbra Streisand called up Agassi. Did she call you first?

PS: (Startled.) No.

DP: They were dating a few years ago at the U.S. Open. I was curious.

PS: I want someone a little younger than that.

DP: You don't want someone in their 50's?

PS: No. She's what I call a pitching wedge. **She looks good from about 150 yards away.** (Both laugh.)

DP: There's that personality. There it is.

DP: What is your dream foursome?

PS: Nicklaus, Jim Carrey, for a little humor because Nicklaus is a serious guy, am I right?

DP: Yeah. He's boring.

PS: **Yeah, he's boring with 18 majors.** (Laughs.) Nicklaus, Jim Carrey and you, Dan. I want to play **golf** with you.

DP: I've got game.

PS: I've heard you got game.

DP: I've got game you only read about. So you don't want some woman in there?

PS: On the golf course? No. I can't stand waiting for the red tees. Let's play from the back.

DP: Is there one question that stands out that you have been asked by the Wimbledon press?

PS: I think the press over there knows they're not going to get much from me so they don't bother asking.

DP: They wouldn't say are you still dating **Jennifer Aniston?**

PS: No.

DP: Do you know who Jennifer Aniston is?

PS: I do. She's a Greek girl. And I'm Greek.

DP: There you go. I am trying to set you up.

PS: We Greeks stay together.

DP: More impressive: Steffi winning a grand slam and Olympic gold in 1988 or Chrissie Evert winning at least one major for 13 consecutive years.

PS: **Why are we talking about ladies' tennis?** But I will answer the question. I would say Chrissie winning a major every year for 13 years.

DP: That's pretty good.

PS: It's pretty impressive.

DP: You don't want to talk about chicks?

PS: Chicks. **What about Lendl getting to the final of the Open eight straight years?**

DP: Is that more impressive than Chrissie...

PS: Well, we are talking **WNBA and NBA, OK?** (Both laugh.) But to answer your question, your cornball question, Chrissie's 13.

DP: I will watch women's tennis.

PS: Because there's personality.

DP: No. When Steffi would play Monica, there was no personality involved. But I would watch because it was great tennis.

PS: You're right, it is. Say you have Gustavo Kuerten playing Carlos Moya at the French, do you watch?

DP: Not over Seles/Graf.

PS: That's honest. Very honest.

DP: Is there an animal that represents you on the court?

PS: **A mongoose.** That was my nickname from my Junior Davis Cup captain. A mongoose is quick and strong and fast enough to catch a snake.

DP: I am glad you gave a good answer because I thought you would say, "What a dumb question!"

PS: No, that's a great question. **Boring answers come from boring questions.** (In a dullish monotone.) "Out there playing today, Pete, what went through your mind?"

DP: Favorite band.

PS: Pearl Jam. (Pause.) Ever hear of them?

DP: Yeah. Eddie Vedder's all right.

PS: He's all right?

DP: He rocks.

PS: He's the king. I'd have to say Pearl Jam, REM, Dave Matthews Band. But Pearl Jam is my...I met them at a concert in Florida. I must say Eddie Vedder was the only guy I've met that I was a little bit in awe of.

DP: Free association. Grass.

PS: Fast.

DP: Clay.

PS: Slippery.

DP: Ace.

PS: Untouchable.

DP: You could have said ecstasy or orgasm.

PS: **We won't go there.**

DP: Venus Williams.

PS: Athletic.

DP: Do you know who Ricky Martin is?

PS: Is he in NASCAR?

DP: He's living "La Vida Loca."

PS: Oh, yeah.

DP: Does anybody hit **the ball so hard you can't see it?**

PS: I can see it but I just can't get to it. Goran Ivanesevic on grass. **When he gets it going, there's not much you can do. Unreturnable.**

DP: What would you do to make the sport more popular?

PS: I would cut half the tournaments. I would change the ranking system. And I would make sure that me and Agassi play in the finals of every Grand Slam.

DAN PATRICK   TONY GWYNN

I don't see any skinny guys

Tony Gwynn and I had a great conversation in 1998 at the NBA Finals in Utah. He was a two-sport star in college and remains a real student of both basketball and baseball, but I was talking to the guy who I consider to be the best hitter of my generation. Having the opportunity to tap into that was an amazing experience. It was fascinating just to listen to him, because I was learning so much. Not that he was all business; he likes to laugh as much as anyone I know, but he also takes his craft more seriously than anyone I know.

When we chatted later that summer for this interview, I was approaching Tony as someone who knows his whole career. Today, we know him primarily as a singles hitter, a guy with 3,000 hits. But he used to steal a lot of bases and play Gold Glove defense. He was a great athlete in right field. Maybe more than in any other interview, I had a bunch of questions that I personally wanted to know the answers to. It took a while before I referred to my research. So pardon my indulgence here, but I'm a father. I needed stuff to tell my kids about hitting and took the opportunity to learn from the master.

DP: Settle this one for all of us innocent bystanders.
Is the ball juiced?
TG: No. The ball's not juiced, period. Every time someone gets off to a good start hitting home runs, they say the ball is juiced. If they mean that the ball is harder than it was thirty years ago, that's probably true.

DP: So it's harder, not juiced?

TG: Yes. When they say it's juiced, what do they mean? They're making them exactly the same way. It just may be wound tighter. Maybe. But juiced? No. Give the players some credit. I mean thirty

doing what I am doing.

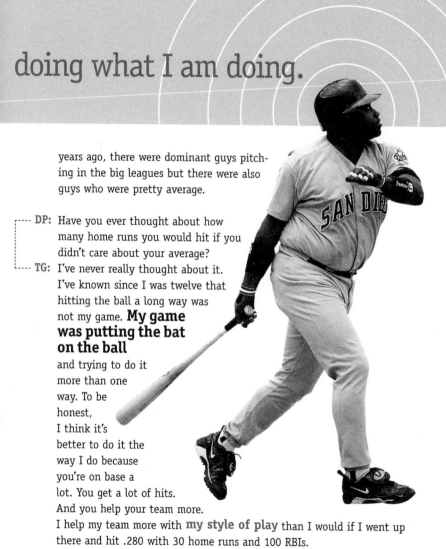

years ago, there were dominant guys pitching in the big leagues but there were also guys who were pretty average.

DP: Have you ever thought about how many home runs you would hit if you didn't care about your average?

TG: I've never really thought about it. I've known since I was twelve that hitting the ball a long way was not my game. **My game was putting the bat on the ball** and trying to do it more than one way. To be honest, I think it's better to do it the way I do because you're on base a lot. You get a lot of hits. And you help your team more. I help my team more with **my style of play** than I would if I went up there and hit .280 with 30 home runs and 100 RBIs.

DP: Is it a compliment to be called **"old school?"**

TG: Yes. Definitely.

DP: Give me some guys who are old school.

TG: Mark Grace is definitely old school. Roger Clemens. Barry Larkin. Mark McGwire, believe it or not, is a throwback, old-school type player.

DP: Can you be young and be old school?

TG: **Scott Rolen of the Phillies.** To me, he's an old-schooler. Every ball he hits he's flying down that line. Ground ball to pitcher. Boom, he's gone. He's aggressive and he slides into bases hard. **He plays the game the way it was meant to be played.**

DP: Name three showoffs.

TG: **Rickey Henderson.** When he was here, when they announced his name he was still in the on-deck circle. He played it with a little flair, a little mustard. I could get in trouble for this one but I think **Craig Biggio** has a little hot dog in him, a little bit of showmanship. He gets to the plate and he has to fix his bat, fix his helmet, tighten his batting gloves, put his pants leg down in his shoe. Then he steps into the box and he's got to touch his pants on the side and touch his helmet again. He's got a little of it in him. But he plays hard, so you can deal with it. Three would be **Chuckie Carr.** I don't know if he's playing now. But Chuckie Carr was a hot dog.

DP: He's playing somewhere. It may not be in the majors but...

TG: He was the biggest hot dog I've seen since I've been in the big leagues. He'd hit .240 or .250 but...

DP: He had the strut of a .400 hitter.

TG: **The mustard was dripping off Chuck Carr. With the other guys, it was just a little bit on their pants.**

DP: When I go to Wrigley, **I sit in the bleachers.** And I heard some things they said to Barry Bonds. Here's a future Hall of Famer and I cringed.

TG: Then you know what I got to listen to. It's probably twice as bad in right field. But don't get me wrong. They have a healthy respect for you. **But their job is to take your mind off of what you are doing. And they are good at it.**

DP: Describe the feeling of getting a hit.

TG: For me it's not just getting a hit but doing it right. It's going to the plate with an idea, with a game plan, and then executing it. Sometimes, it doesn't end up a hit, just a line drive or a hard ground ball. But just going up to the plate with a game plan and you want to execute it and you do, that's the best part of the game. If you get a hit, that's a bonus.

DP: Have you ever gotten a hit and been dissatisfied?

TG: Oh, yeah. Many times.

DP: Have you ever lined out and been happy?

TG: High-fiving on the bench? Yep. As hitters we want to get hits, but sometimes you have to set your sights a little lower. You go to the plate and you want to execute what you're trying to do. It might not end up on a hit but the more times you do it right, the better your chances are going to be.

DP: What's a worse feeling: getting caught looking at a third strike or swinging at a third strike?

TG: Swinging. Because if you get caught looking, you can say to yourself, "If I had swung at that, I would have hit it." When I get caught looking, it's probably a good pitch and I was fooled on it or I was looking for something else. At least, when you swing, even if you looked bad like I have this year, at least you made an attempt at it.

DP: Give me **three teammates you could beat in a footrace.** No questions asked.

TG: Probably Wally Joyner because his leg is messed up.

DP: Oh, so you are going to take advantage of a cripple?

TG: You said no questions, so ... that's one. I think I could beat Carlos Hernandez and Greg Myers. So **both of our catchers and our crippled first baseman.**

DP: Do you have to remind these younger guys that you once stole 56 bases?

TG: We were just talking about that. I said to them, "You guys act like I can't do anything anymore. Did you know I stole 56 bases one year?" And they said, "What year?" I said, "1987." They laughed and told me, "That was 11 years ago!" And I said, "Well, I'm two for two this year." And I told them that you have to use your brain sometimes. **It isn't just using your speed, you have to use your brain.**

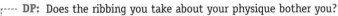

DP: Does the ribbing you take about your physique bother you?

TG: It used to bother me a lot. My line used to be, **"I don't see any skinny guys doing what I am doing."** Now it doesn't bother me as much but every now and then it does. Like the fans in Wrigley, that's the butt of all their jokes.

DP: No pun intended.

TG: Exactly. As long as I play, I'm going to get ragged about how I look.

How big my stomach is.

My patent leather shoes. Something.

DP: What current NBA player reminds you of you during your college basketball days?

TG: **Tyus Edney.** But he's faster than I was and shoots better. **But he reminded me of me.**

DP: Three pitchers you would go to dinner with, past or present.

TG: **Sandy Koufax. Don Newcombe.** And to name someone from today's game, Denny Neagle.

DP: Would you go to learn or to be entertained.

TG: With Koufax and Newcombe, it would be to learn. Because they aren't playing anymore. In Neagle's case, it would be both. I want to find out how he keeps getting me out. But he is hilarious, too.

DP: Can you learn more from watching a game or talking about it?

TG: For what I do, **I can learn more talking about it than watching it.** The game itself, for me, is not going to vary much. There's little things that you can learn about the game, learn about preparation, from talking about it. I've had the chance to sit down and talk to Ted Williams, Stan Musial, Rod Carew, **Pete Rose.** I've been able to pick their brains to find out what they did to prepare to do the things that they did.

DP: Would you hate to be a pitcher facing Tony Gwynn?

TG: No. I would love the opportunity. Because I don't think it's that hard. If you mix it up, keep me off balance, you have a good chance of getting me out. It's that simple. But if I'm going good, **I don't get fooled very often and generally when I swing, I hit it. You gotta make a good pitch.**

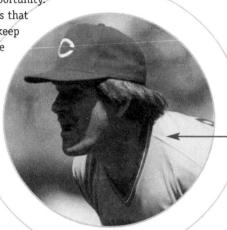

DP: Have you ever sneaked a peak at the catcher's sign?

TG: While I was hitting? No. I don't want to know what's coming.

I would rather trust what I see.

If my eyes see something, I want to react to that. I don't want anybody giving me signs. Now, after guys read this, catchers around the league will be telling me every pitch. The consensus in this league is just throw it down the middle and let him get himself out. Because if it's out, he's going to left and if it's in he's going to right. If you throw it down the middle, he might confuse himself and get himself out. And a lot of people actually believe that.

DAN PATRICK   **TOM GLAVINE**

I wouldn't know if chicks

(W)ith Randy Johnson, you can watch every third or fourth pitch in an at-bat and still see the strikeout. He's become much better at the mental side of the game, but will probably always rely on his ability to blow people away. Not so with Tom Glavine. He compels you to watch every pitch to see what he is up to. He's a pitcher, not a thrower, and always has been.

Peter Gammons once told me that whenever he is looking for a good quote, he goes to Tom Glavine. So I thought he'd be a good subject for this format. He had some fun and let me bully him into a corner a few times, and still gave me an answer. Glavine's experience in two sports also lends a fresh perspective to his take on things.

Glavine has been there since the beginning of this great Atlanta run when he was one of the better players on a couple of bad teams. As a result, the Braves of the 1990s have taken on Tom Glavine's personality. Glavine is a quiet guy, but on the mound he has a steely determination. He has been a very good pitcher on a very good team, but there always seems to be someone who overshadows him. I don't really think he has been given his due. But you'll hear more about that from me than you ever will from him.

DP: As a Bostonian, any thoughts on the new Fenway plans? Does it hurt you that there is not going to be Fenway as we know it some day?

TG: Ummmm. No.

DP: You don't care?

TG: It's not that I don't care. Those places are awesome but to me, once the Garden went... I mean if the Garden can go, anything can go. I think because of that I am a little less shocked by that kind of stuff. The way things are nowadays you understand that it's probably a business decision more than anything else.

dig it or not.

DP: The ball is not juiced. That's what we've been told.

TG: (Laughs.) Ummm.

DP: Does that mean it's wound tighter, then?

TG: I think it is definitely wound tighter. How much that makes a difference, I don't know. I can pick up certain balls and feel that they are harder than others.

DP: What makes more of a difference: The way the balls are wound or the way the strike zone is?

TG: Do I have to answer that question?

DP: (Laughs.)

TG: All right. Probably the ball.

DP: So you are being politically correct.

TG: No. Maybe a little bit. But I see too many guys hitting home runs to the opposite field that shouldn't be doing it. I don't think that has much to do with the strike zone. That's the ball. And the ballparks. The new parks are hitters' parks.

DP: Does it scare you to see someone like Greg Maddux struggle?

TG: I don't think what Greg and I are going through really scares you. I just think that he is going through a stretch where things aren't quite right.

And so am I. But always in the back of your mind is that any given day could be the last day. I'm more fearful of what happened to Tony Saunders than I am of what is happening to me and Greg right now. **I'm more fearful of going out there and blowing my arm out and that's the end of it.**

DP: Who is the **best reliever** you ever saw?

TG: Probably **Dennis Eckersley.**

He had that tremendous ability to throw hard and still locate the ball. And some of the stats he put up are just mind-boggling. He may not be the most dominating guy in terms of, **"Hey, here it is and you can't hit it."** But, in terms of being able to throw the ball where he wanted to and the minuscule amount of walks he had compared to his saves, you'd have to say he was one of the best. His consistency over the long haul was amazing.

DP: It's almost like Eck said: **"Now you see it, now you don't."** Maddux, too.

TG: You are seeing something. What you are seeing is the early part of a pitch. Those guys have such late movement. You may recognize it first but when it comes into the hitting zone, that is when it starts to move.

DP: You were drafted by the Kings. **You could have played with Wayne Gretzky.**

TG: My line always is that his career would have been forever changed if we played together. He would have had to move to left wing. I was a center.

DP: I think he would have done it.

TG: I think he could have made the adjustment better than me.

DP: **Should managers wear uniforms?**

TG: Yeah. In baseball, they are as much a part of the team as the players are. When those guys get on the field and argue with an umpire, it looks a whole lot better than it would if they were in a suit and a tie.

DP: But there are some managers who don't belong in a uniform and you know it.

TG: Oh, absolutely. But don't make me name them.

DP: You wouldn't name a manager or two that might look better in a suit?

TG: I'd rather not.

DP: Come on! (Both laugh.) **I had no problem prying things out of Maddux and David Cone.**

TG: Well, of course you didn't.

DP: Greg Maddux?

TG: Oh, well. Good point.

DP: If you could be one pitcher for a day who would it be?

TG: Probably... (Long pause.) Smoltzie.

DP: Why?

TG: He throws hard so he can challenge guys with his fastball. And he can make guys look ridiculous with his breaking ball. I can't do that.

DP: Best players in baseball.

TG: **Griffey, Bonds, Gwynn.**

DP: You think Gwynn still is?

TG: I don't care what he does in his last year or two. He's been the best hitter in our era. I don't see a lot of American League guys. McGwire and Sosa, too.

DP: As a pitcher, was too much made of McGwire/Sosa last year?

TG: No. That's a record that stood for a long, long time. A lot of people probably had it down as one that would never get broken. Obviously, what made it exciting was having two guys doing it in one year. It was good for baseball. Anybody who didn't see that was looking at the wrong thing. **Those two guys pretty much wiped out whatever bad feelings were left about baseball.**

DP: **How do you pitch McGwire?**

TG: With Mac, you really have to make him conscious inside because he has such great coverage away. Obviously, **if he extends his arms, he's going to kill you.** I probably try to make him as conscious inside as

I do anybody. And just continuously change speeds on him. If you go in, you try to go in above his hands where he hopefully can't extend himself.

DP: Does your wife mind that chicks dig the long ball?

TG: She was a little upset at first when she found out that **Heather Locklear**

was going to be in it. But she quickly got over that. She's not worried about it with me because I only have one career home run. I wouldn't know if they dig it or not.

DP: **Last guy that homered off you that had no business homering.**

TG: Livan Hernandez.

DP: Is there a guy who owns you that shouldn't?

TG: Yeah. Another guy from their team. A backup catcher named Redmond. I have thrown everything but the <u>kitchen sink</u> at him.

When I make a bad pitch, he hits it hard. When I make a good pitch, he bloops it in somewhere.

DP: Which NHL player has your game?

TG: I was more like a Gretzky or a **Jaromir Jagr** but obviously not that good. Is Mike Modano that kind of player?

DP: Yeah.

TG: A scoring-assist kind of guy. I didn't get into corners and muck it up.

DP: So you were a pretty boy?

TG: Yeah...I guess. I mean I didn't shy away from it if it came my way. But my job was to get in front of the net and score goals.

DP: **Would you groove a pitch for a friend?**

TG: Depends.

DP: Give me a scenario and who you would do it for.

TG: Let's say I have a 10-1 lead, late in the game. And I have a buddy on the other team who is struggling to stay in the big leagues. He really needs a hit.

DP: So Jeff Blauser.

TG: (Laughs.) Yeah, you can use Blauser.

DP: So Blauser's struggling. What do you do?

TG: I might work the outer half or inner half rather than outer or inner corner.

DP: So you wouldn't exactly serve one up to him?

TG: I'm not going to throw one right down the middle. You have to keep some sense of the integrity of the game. But I might throw him a fastball in what might be a change-up count for me.

DP: But you wouldn't let him know.

TG: Yeah. I wouldn't tell him.

DP: Are pitchers athletes?

TG: Absolutely.

DP: Mark Grace says no.

TG: That's the biggest fallacy in sports. I think there is a handful of pitchers who give the rest of us a bad name. I would venture to say that most of us pitchers are better athletes than most of the players.

DP: Who are some pitchers who make you say, "We're better than that."

TG: You're stumping me. I can't think.

DP: I'm letting you get away with this. There has to be someone.

TG: OK. How about one of our guys, Kevin McGlinchy?

DP: Kevin McGlinchy. You're kind of taking the easy way out, aren't you?

TG: Yeah, but that's OK. (Both laugh.)

DP: I thought you would just name somebody who...

TG: I probably could, but I can't think off the top of my head.

DP: Who's the fat toad on the Yankees?

TG: Irabu.

DP: Would you say that Hideki Irabu and his physique make pitchers proud to be pitchers?

TG: Probably.

DP: Come on!

TG: Well, I don't see Hideki that much. I don't know if he can hit or field.

DP: He can't do anything. He can barely cover first base. That's why Steinbrenner...

TG: Put him down!!!

DP: Man. Here I was rooting for you to get out of this slump and...

TG: You still are!! (Both laugh.) We go way back.

DAN PATRICK

JULIE FOUDY

I'm Shaq. I choke in

Off the field, Julie Foudy seems like she'd be a flamboyant crowd-pleaser on the field. But in reality, she provides steady play and veteran leadership. And I think her validation is not the same as other athletes'. She has the right perspective—and a great sense of humor.

Still, I was a little apprehensive about interviewing Julie. I had heard from several people that she'd be great. But the conventional wisdom is that if you interview a female athlete, she needs to be particularly well known. And if you interview a female soccer player, she should be Mia Hamm.

Well, you can score it Word of Mouth: 1 and Conventional Wisdom: 0. Julie was lively and entertaining from the get-go. She had worked at ESPN and had a really good sense of what we were trying to do. She even proved prophetic in talking at length about uniforms and the whole notion of what would happen if a woman ripped off her shirt at the end of a game, like so many men do. Brandi Chastain provided the answer, but Julie had asked the question months earlier. And she was dead-on about who could help her Lakers, too.

●

DP: Why don't women throw their shirts into the crowd after a soccer game like the men do?

JF: I've tried to push that. I say, **"Come on, we're wearing sports bras."** It would bring in more fans. But they didn't go for it.

DP: Does sex sell in World Cup?

JF: (Laughs.) We could prove it if we could take off our jerseys. We'd sell out every stadium. Make it a rule for every team. Only in beach volleyball, I guess.

DP: Do Americans get soccer?

JF: No, I don't think as a country we do. We may eventually. My parents' generation didn't play soccer. So when they are watching it they say,

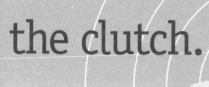

the clutch.

"What's offsides again?" Seriously. They are clueless. But this next generation, with so many playing the game, at least they understand the game a bit.

DP: Do they understand how good you are?

JF: No. (Laughs.) I can have a terrible game or a great game and they say, **"Honey, we just thought you played great."**

DP: Is that frustrating?

JF: No. I love it.

DP: Do you like that they don't really know?

JF: I love it like that. They are very supportive but they are not obsessed soccer people. I had to convince my dad for the first Women's World Cup that he needed to be there. He says (in a deep voice), "Well, that's a busy time for me, honey." (Laughs.) "Got a lot of work. Can't just take three weeks off." (Laughs.) I said, "Dad, this is the World Cup." He didn't even know what the World Cup was. I said, "You should go. You won't be disappointed. Just trust your youngest."

DP: What is the difference in talent level on the **U.S. men's team versus the women's team?**

JF: I think our men don't get the credit they deserve. People say, "Oh, the women are always winning. The men aren't winning." But the men are in a totally different situation. They started off late in the game, relatively speaking, compared to the rest of the world. Soccer is the thing in the rest of the world. People live and breathe it. And die for it.

DP: Literally.

JF: Yes. So when the men play, they have to go against basketball, football and baseball. I think they lose a lot of athletes that way. And there is just not the same passion that there is around the world for it. They are fighting that all the time. These people around the world are playing it right out of the womb. And here that's just not the case. With us, it's a different story. **Women's soccer isn't as accepted in other parts of the world.** We're kind of the leaders, which is ironic.

DP: Tell me something about **Mia Hamm** that I shouldn't know.

JF: (Laughs.) **Mia? She's a closet freak.**

DP: She's a closet freak?

JF: I think she wears pink teddies to bed. She was also pushing for that as our uniform.

DP: So she's the Victoria's Secret one out of the bunch?

JF: No, that's Carla Overbeck.

DP: So Mia is a closet freak.

JF: I get all this crap from reporters about Mia being so shy. "She never talks."

DP: Oh, yeah, I saw her at the Jimmy V classic. **She's a little smarty.**

JF: Yeah, a smart-ass. I have to smack her around sometimes to keep her in place. But she's a great player and more importantly she's a solid person. All of the acclaim she has received could be a problem on a team

sport but with us, she's the first one we tell, **"Grab the water. Who are you, the <u>Queen of England? Get over here.</u>"**
(Laughs.)

DP: With the language barrier, is there any trash talking?

JF: No.

DP: Come on. You have to have trash talking.

JF: Mia is a good trash talker. She always denies it but she is.

DP: Give me a typical one.

JF: You don't so much with the opponents as the referees. Because they usually speak English. And that can get you in trouble.

DP: But Mia will talk trash. With whom?

JF: The refs. Because she gets abused out there pretty much. When you are a forward, you are always playing with your back to the goal. She's always getting on the refs about getting more calls and protecting her a little more.

DP: So she's a crybaby?

JF: (Laughs.) She's like Karl Malone. I was so happy to see them lose.

DP: Why?

JF: **I'm a huge Laker fan and they kick the Lakers out every year.**

DP: How can you be a Laker fan?

JF: I know. I know.

DP: Well, explain it.

JF: I am disappointed in them. But I grew up watching Magic Johnson and Kareem, Cooper, Worthy. What a great team. Back then. In the '60s or whenever it was. (Laughs.)

DP: What's the problem with the Lakers?

JF: No leader. Shaq can't do it.

DP: What do you suggest? Somebody has to go?

JF: **I think so. Or they need to get Phil Jackson. Could you work on that, Dan?**

DP: If you were going to match up Lakers with your World Cup team, who would Mia be and who would you be?

JF: (Laughs.) I'm Shaq. Choke in the clutch. **Why do they insist on giving him the ball with one minute left? They just foul him.**

DP: I know.

JF: I get so angry.

DP: Mia is...

JF: More like Kobe. She's got the flair, she can finish. She can drive the lane.

DP: What athlete would you be excited to meet?

JF: Jerry Rice. **I love Jerry Rice.** He's been so solid and consistent for so many years. And he just does his job and doesn't have to show a lot of flash. He just gets it done. I was pretty excited to meet Billie Jean King. She's my hero.

DP: Because she beat Bobby Riggs?

JF: No. **I love Billie Jean King** because she has done so much for women's athletics. We have been through a lot off the field with this sport. And I just love how she still helps her sport but she shares her insights with the other sports.

DP: Are you supposed to be **celibate** during this time?

JF: (Laughs.) It's the men's team that lays those rules down. We were talking about that the other day. That's one place where we tell Tony [DeCicco] off limits. Too personal, Coach.

DP: How's he going to know? A little spring in your step?

JF: (Laughs.) **Coming down to breakfast smiling. Guilty.**

DP: If **Monica Lewinsky** was your teammate...

JF: Did somebody tell you my feeling about her?

DP: What position would she play?

JF: Fat water girl on the side of the bench. (Laughs.) God. Don't even put her on the bench. (Mocking, high voice) I want to apologize to the country and Hillary for having sex with the president. Hee-hee-hee-hee. I feel so terrible about this. Hee-hee-hee-hee. Could you believe that interview? And no one hammered her?

DP: I got my Mia Hamm Barbie doll. Do you wish you had one?

JF: No. She got a lot of abuse for that. Have you seen the commercial?

DP: No. I'm still getting over the one with Michael Jordan. The one I got was not anatomically correct with Mia Hamm.

JF: I couldn't even look at it, to be honest.

DP: **My Barbie looks like Pamela Lee.**

JF: But that's Mia, last time I checked. I have seen her in the locker room, you know.

DP: Last CD you bought? Britney Spears?

JF: Ricky Martin.

DP: "Livin' La Vida Loca!" Is that your locker room music?

JF: He is a team favorite.

DP: What is the **first thing you do when you get to a hotel room?**

JF: Take the bedspread off the bed. You've seen those "20/20"s. It's not good. You have to get that thing off. Thank God we are staying at a place where they put a sheet over the blanket. I travel too much. Can't touch the blanket either.

DP: That's because you know how you are on the road?

JF: Yeah. One of the rookies had her face on the bedspread and I said, "Do you not know?" (Laughs.) **What about you and your boyfriend when he visits you?** (Laughs.)

DP: I have three little daughters. Don't tell me that.

JF: Three little girls. How old?

DP: Eleven months. She's crying now. And four and six, they are at school. My seven-year-old son is at school, too.

JF: You're going to have little soccer players. Then you'll like it.

DP: I am trying to get one of my daughters into it. But I think the four-year-old will play. She loves to go out and bang it around. She's tough.

JF: They start them young.

DP: I can't do that. **Let them be kids. It's sad.**

JF: I lost years. Didn't start until I was seven. They start them at five. I say to myself, "That's two years, dammit." (Laughs.) People are freaks about it.

DP: When is the ideal time to start them?

JF: **When they want to is the ideal time.**

I don't know if it was officially

I have known Barry Sanders since the day in 1988 that he announced he was leaving Oklahoma State after his Heisman-winning junior year. While he was leaving school early, he was late for the press conference. And while he doesn't relish the media spotlight, he had a good reason for keeping us waiting. His car broke down.

Since then, I have been to his house (very understated), played some hoops with him (not as good as he thinks) and met his parents (great people). Barry has become one of the few people that I view as a friend more than just another athlete. He knows that if he has 150 yards and two touchdowns that I'll still mention the fumble. What are friends for?

Barry and I chatted during the 1998 season. He's still no publicity hound, but as you'll see, Barry does not evade questions the way he does tacklers. He's not afraid of anything. Not Reggie White. Not John Randle. Not even the ghost of Jim Brown.

Since our conversation, Barry abruptly retired just before the start of the 1999 season. I think he'll be back. We'll see.

DP: Do you have a deep desire to play another position?

BS: Yes. I have a deep desire to play cornerback. I'd be a good one.

DP: Why?

BS: Because...uh...the last time you spoon-fed this one to me.

DP: I asked you about Deion Sanders.

BS: You said, "Is it because you can't tackle?"

DP: I mean, you don't like to be hit, so why would you want to hit someone?

BS: That's why I'd make a perfect corner.

DP: So your idol, your prototypical corner, would be Deion Sanders.

sleep. Or if I was dozing.

BS: (Laughs.) **I don't know about that. I don't want to rip Deion up like that.**

DP: But he doesn't have to tackle anybody... right?

BS: Naw, man. Every now and then he'll grab somebody's shoestring.

DP: But he's never laid a hit on you and you said, "Wow, that hurt!"

BS: No, he's not going to do that.

DP: So you're right. You would be the perfect defensive back. You would look good. You could keep up with the receivers and have somebody come over and deliver the blows, right?

BS: (Laughs.) Okay.

DP: So no desire to be the quarterback or the wide receiver?

BS: Naw. That's the easy part.

DP: Are you the best athlete in your family?

BS: My father would immediately say he was the best athlete in the family.

DP: Even at age 61 he'd say that?

BS: Oh, yeah. **He'd say I was slowly closing the gap.**

DP: Do you ever think you'll be as good in your dad's eyes as Jim Brown?

BS: Noooo. Not even close. No one has ever been in the same ballpark as Jim Brown, in my father's eyes.

DP: Does he remind you of this all the time?

BS: No matter what topic you're talking about. You can walk in and say, "Daddy, how are you doing today?" And he'll say, **"You'll never be as good as Jim Brown."**

DP: That's tough. Have you asked your dad what it will take to surpass Jim Brown as his favorite running back?

BS: No. Because if I ask him that, it would just give him a reason to tell me why I'll never be as good as Jim Brown.

DP: Favorite running backs to watch?

BS: The Bus, **Jerome Bettis.** He's pretty nifty for a big man. **Terrell Davis.** He's explosive and he's like a ticking bomb for the defense. It's just a matter of time before he's going to do something exciting.

DP: What kind of training camp roommate is Herman Moore?

BS: Oh, man. You don't want to room with Herman Moore. He's always watching these gory movies. He's got the TV turned up as high as it goes. He wants to feel like he's in a theater. And he watches videos that are banned from TV. **They should really keep a close eye on him.**

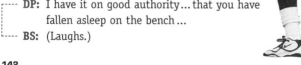

DP: Three best end zone celebrations.

BS: Billy (White Shoes) Johnson, Butch Johnson and Deion Sanders.

DP: **What exactly is Deion doing?**

BS: I'm not sure. But it looks kind of cool.

DP: I have it on good authority...that you have fallen asleep on the bench...

BS: (Laughs.)

DP: While the defense is on the field.

BS: (Still laughing.) Oh, man. I was dreaming about the next series.

DP: Well, you can dream with your eyes open, you know?

BS: But you get a fuller effect when you're unconscious and your eyes are closed.

DP: You actually admit that you fell asleep on the bench during an NFL game?

BS: Back a few years ago we didn't have a very exciting defense.

DP: So they were out there a while?

BS: Yeah.

DP: Do you remember when you fell asleep? Or has this happened a couple of times?

BS: Who remembers falling asleep?

DP: I didn't know if it was once or ten times. And Herman Moore came over to wake you up.

BS: I can't believe he said that!

DP: At least you admit it.

BS: Well, I don't know if it was officially sleep. Or if I was dozing. There's a fine line there.

DP: Can you imagine if Mike Ditka was your coach and he found out you fell asleep on the bench?

DP: Is there a coach you couldn't play for?

BS: I don't know. My father. I don't know if I could play for him.

DP: You could play for Ditka? Vince Lombardi?

BS: I don't know. I don't know what Mike is like on a daily basis. I don't need the yelling and screaming type. If he's the yelling and screaming type, we'd have to work out some kind of agreement. **We'd just get together on Sunday.** And maybe I'd just practice separately during the week.

DP: Yeah, I think Coach would go for that arrangement.

DP: Do you still do your own laundry?

BS: Yes. Everyone does their own laundry. Of course.

DP: I don't.

BS: Well, I'm not married. Yet. So I still have to do my own laundry.

DP: Oh, I see. Once you get married, you'll just let your wife do the laundry. That's a good way to attract a woman. **"I want you to do my laundry."** That's great. Send your cards and letters to Barry Sanders.

BS: That's risky right there.

DP: I know it is.

DP: Are you a showoff?

BS: Not really.

DP: Because you often find that guys who are shy off the field are demonstrative on it. It's almost like an alter ego. Is that the way you are? Or is it just your style that makes it look like you are showing off?

BS: Let me go talk to my psychiatrist and get back to you on this one. **You went way out there on this one. Way out there, man.**

DP: Has anybody tried to get up in your face on the football field?

BS: People try all the time.

DP: Who does? What do they say to you?

BS: Not to recall any names, but you hear stuff all the time...

DP: I like names.

BS: About what you're not going to do, like, "It's not happening today."

DP: What does Warren Sapp say?

BS: Warren just gets up and does a dance. Hardy Nickerson used to talk when he first came to Tampa. He's more mellowed out now. And he may do a late hit or punch you on the bottom of the pile. You know who talks a lot? John Randle. He's just flat-out crazy. For one, he has his face painted with this warrior paint. It's not just eye black. It's actual war-paint type stuff. Like he's going into a battle. So he looks goofy anyway. He'll get in your face and say all kinds of craziness. He's going to rip you apart, this, that and the other.

DP: Sosa or McGwire.

BS: McGwire.

DP: No explanation?

BS: Well, Big Mac. I mean the first time I heard of Sammy Sosa was this year. I'm not a huge baseball guy, but I had heard of Big Mac forever.

DP: If McGwire were going to play football, what position?

BS: Linebacker. Definitely linebacker.

DP: Grass or artificial turf?

BS: Grass.

DP: Aren't you better on Astroturf than on natural grass?

BS: It depends on what I'm doing.

DP: How about running the football?

BS: Not necessarily.

DP: You're faster on turf, aren't you?

BS: Since we all play on the same surface, **it doesn't do me any good to be faster on artificial turf, because we're all faster.**

DP: So your style isn't better suited to artificial surfaces, the cuts, the stops, the starts?

BS: Not at all. I think I can make better cuts on grass. It's safer anyway.

DP: Super Bowl victory or all-time rushing record?

DP: Super Bowl.

DP: They talk about guys like **Gretzky, Bird and Magic** having a sense of where people are going to be, what was going to happen in advance.

BS: I think they're making it up. Those guys were just good, you know.

DP: So you're not thinking out there?

BS: I'm not totally brain dead out there. That's why you practice every day. You develop certain habits, get your timing down, learn how to read defenses. You learn how to read blocks. And sometimes you improvise. I'm not psychic and it's not like I'm going full speed and everybody else is in slow motion.

DP: Any defensive player you have feared? Maybe not outwardly, because you can't admit something like that. But inwardly you say, I have to stay away from this guy or these guys.

BS: **Mike Singletary.**
Lawrence Taylor.
They were getting older but I was still intimidated by their presence. **Ronnie Lott.**
Guys like that.

DP: Is it okay for guys to run out of bounds instead of getting hit?

BS: (Laughs.) It depends on who's chasing them out of bounds. That's where the thinking part comes in.

DP: The most flattering thing another player has said about you?

BS: My first year, after we played the Giants. It was my first start. Lawrence Taylor came up to me and said, "If they get you a fullback and a tight end, you'll be unstoppable."

I'd say I could throw it as good as

(I) first met Dan Marino at a Hootie and the Blowfish concert. Now, Dan knew I was from Cincinnati and he's from Pittsburgh, so there's a built-in rivalry there. When he saw me, he came right up and hit me in the sternum with the back of his hand. Hard. It made a thud. He wanted to go toe to toe with me, a little verbal sparring on our regional differences. I went right at him and we had a good time, talking about everything but football.

Afterward, I think he felt bad about challenging me that way. (I have to admit I was expecting a sort of "Hi, Dan. How are you?" exchange. For both of us.) He sent me a couple of bottles of wine with a note of apology for being in my face so much that day. And his phone number.

So I called him and was all over him. I left him a message along the lines of, "You are so sensitive! I don't want your wine. I don't take gifts from athletes. And I'm still going to rip you on *SportsCenter*. Don't you ever think you got to me." He got the biggest kick out of that. I forgot to mention that I would take Tony Perez over Willie Stargell any day of the week. Maybe next time I see him.

DP: If you hear any strange noises during this interview, it's my five-week-old daughter.

DM: All right, man. Congratulations. First baby?

DP: No. Fourth.

DM: Wow. Well, you're like me now.

DP: I caught up to you. Can I promise her that you will win a Super Bowl in her lifetime?

DM: Ummm...yeah. Promise her but cross your fingers.

DP: Do you look at your individual honors and maybe cherish them more now that you are in the twilight of your career?

DM: Yes. You do look at them now and understand that in the history of the NFL, I was the guy who threw the most touchdown passes. And you do cherish them a little more. For me the most important record is the touchdown passes because it's scoring points and helping your team win. To me, though, I wouldn't give up a 16-year career of being consistent. That, in some ways, is more important than some of the records that I have. **And as far as giving some of them up to win a Super Bowl, I would for sure.**

DP: You just wouldn't give up the touchdown one.

DM: Well, that one is important to me. I think it's pretty special.

DP: Can you think of one game when you purposely ran it up? When you realized you could do something personally, individually?

DM: In 1984, there were times when I could have thrown for more than I did but Coach Shula shut us off from throwing the football. There was a game in St. Louis and I think we threw for **300 yards** in the first half.

I think I threw **four touchdowns** that day and I could maybe have gotten **six or seven.** There were a couple of times that year when Coach Shula did that.

DP: In 1984, you had to feel you were the best quarterback in the game.

DM: I think I felt that on any given day I could play as well as anybody. But there are a lot of good players who have played well for so long. I think you would be selfish to say you were the best. Joe Montana won the Super Bowl that year. He was pretty damn good, too. So, you feel it inside but it isn't necessarily something you go around telling everybody.

DP: Could you ever be a backup?

DM: Right now, I would not be happy being a backup. But as time goes on … if I was in a position on a team where I could help them win a Super Bowl, as a starter or a backup, and if I felt comfortable with the situation and the people I was around, I would consider it.

DP: Steve Young told me that the definition of a pure passer is a guy who can't run. Are you a pure passer then?

DM: I am not a guy who can run down the field like Steve Young. **I'd say I can throw it as good as anyone who ever played.** One of the better things I've done over the years is make people miss inside the pocket. I move within the pocket but still keep my body in position to throw and make plays.

DP: You're deceptively slow in the pocket?

DM: (Laughs.) That's it! Deceptively slow.

DP: You are not afraid to show your emotions and let somebody know if they've done something wrong. You yell.

DM: I think I can say that over the last five years I haven't yelled at a guy individually for something. Now earlier on, playing with Mark Duper and Mark Clayton, we used to get in fights all the time.

DP: So, what were those conversations like?

DM: Well, there were many times that I would throw a pass at Duper and I didn't like his effort going for the football. **He would respond in certain language about how if I'm getting paid all that money**

I should be able to hit him in the chest with it! We had a relationship that you don't see a lot in today's game because of free agency and guys moving around. We played together for eleven years.

DP: Three teammates, present or former, you could beat in a footrace.

DM: (Laughs.) Bernie Kosar is one for sure. Right now and at any time in his career. I don't think there are many current teammates that I could beat. I'd be close, though. Maybe some of the offensive linemen. Maybe Richmond Webb.

DP: One piece of advice for **Peyton Manning.**

DM: Get a good investment consultant.
(Laughs.) He's going to be a good quarterback for a long time. I think that a lot of the younger quarterbacks should take pride in what they are doing. Also, I don't think that the appreciation of the game and the history of the game is the same with young players now as it was in the past.

DP: I'm sure he does, with his father.

DM: Without a doubt he does. I'm not saying that about him but guys in general. Anyway, the best advice would be to get a good broker.

DP: How many times have you been mistaken for "Baywatch"'s David Hasselhoff?

DM: A few. A handful. Mostly people just say I look like him. They don't come up and ask me if I am him.

DP: Compare and contrast **Jimmy Johnson and Don Shula.**

DM: Very similar in their approach and their desire to win. Both of them are very intense as far as the emotions of winning and losing. Coach Shula and Coach Johnson are also very similar in the amount of preparation that they put into it and what they expect the players to put in each week. Coach Johnson is around the locker room more. You'll see him in the weight room. Coach Shula would be on the field, obviously, then he would be upstairs in the offices and you'd see him in the meeting rooms. You wouldn't see him in the locker room or in the players' lounge.

DP: When do you feel like an old player?

DM: When we talk about playing in college. And I talk about playing in the 1979 Fiesta Bowl and some of my teammates were in the second grade! Or when my wife tells me, "Dan-O, our oldest son is eleven years old and he's closer in age to some of the rookies than you are."

DP: Do you even try to relate to a younger player?

DM: Sure. The one thing we all have in common is that we play football, and that doesn't change.

DP: When you came into the league who was the player you learned the most from?

DM: Don Strock. When I came in as a rookie, he was a ten-year veteran, played with Griese and other, older veterans, too. You could tell he was a student of the game. Right off the bat, I asked him for his help. And today he is one of my closest friends.

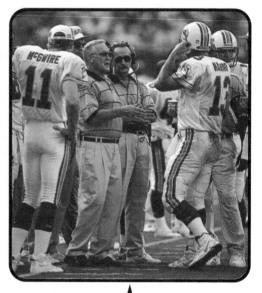

DP: Free association. **Jim Carrey.**

DM: Goofy.

DP: Mark O'Meara.

DM: Solid.

DP: Darius Rucker.

DM: My man.

DP: Don Shula.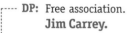

DM: The best.

DP: John Elway.

DM: The best.

DP: You did some color commentating for the World League.

DM: I did twelve games and I think the last four or five I actually got the hang of it. I want to stay involved with football when I'm done playing and that's probably the best way. And **seeing the way coaches have to deal with players these days, I'm not sure I would want to do that.**

DP: When you hear people say that if maybe the Dolphins stopped passing so much, maybe ran a little bit, they would win more. Is that like saying maybe if Michael Jordan would shoot less and pass it around a little bit…

DM: Basketball is different. One guy shooting can have more of an impact. Throwing the football has been what we've done and we've relied on it to win. We've always tried to run the ball. But it has come to the situation where we can't run it and we end up throwing it sixty times in a game. In this league, I don't care who you are, it's difficult to win throwing the ball that often.

DP: What is it with the **NASCAR** craze now?

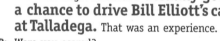

DM: I had always been interested in watching the races but then they wanted me to get involved in the sponsorship. We looked at it for about a year and kind of got hooked. **I actually got a chance to drive Bill Elliott's car at Talladega.** That was an experience.

DP: Were you scared?

DM: I was nervous. We did ten laps the first time and about twelve the second. I was in his second McDonald's car. We did a few laps together. Got up to about a 165 average.

DP: Does your wife know about this?

DM: Yeah, she came. She might have been nervous around the time I got over 150. I guess she figured that if I was going to hit the wall she wanted to be there.

DP: Just to identify you?

DM: Yeah. But, hey, I can take a hit.

DAN PATRICK **MARK GRACE**

If you don't get caught, it's

Ⓜ️ark Grace is a rarity. A legitimate star who has remained a regular guy. You just don't hear negatives about him. Every time I have been around him, there is no air, no stuffiness about him. You ask him a question, he gives you an answer and worries about the fallout later. And I'm not even sure he bothers to worry about it. As a result, he is great clubhouse guy — an honest clubhouse guy who keeps the team front and center.

Gracie is also the quintessential "ballplayer." There are many faces and memories that we will take from baseball in the 1990s and Gracie is certainly one of them. Now he is not necessarily a preeminent player but a guy who just goes out every day and does it. You look up and he's batting .300. And you know who had more hits in the 1990s than any other player? Mark Grace. Even with that kind of performance, he remains unassuming.

Gracie's legacy with the Cubs will be just like Don Mattingly's with the Yankees: They never made it to the World Series; and both Grace and Mattingly rank just below the greatest players in their teams' histories; but they played every day at a high level and did more than their share to uphold — even advance — two of baseball's proudest traditions.

DP: Some of your friends have described you as an idiot savant. Do you care to explain?

MG: Well, the only thing I'm near being an idiot savant on is the state capitals, of course. I can name the capital of any state in the country lickety split and give you great trivia questions about state capitals. But I don't think I could tell you who the Secretary of State is. I really know the important things.

DP: Capital of New Hampshire?

MG: Concord.

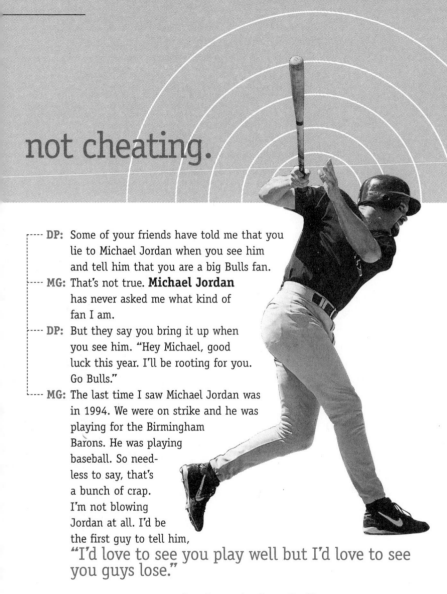

not cheating.

DP: Some of your friends have told me that you lie to Michael Jordan when you see him and tell him that you are a big Bulls fan.

MG: That's not true. **Michael Jordan** has never asked me what kind of fan I am.

DP: But they say you bring it up when you see him. "Hey Michael, good luck this year. I'll be rooting for you. Go Bulls."

MG: The last time I saw Michael Jordan was in 1994. We were on strike and he was playing for the Birmingham Barons. He was playing baseball. So needless to say, that's a bunch of crap. I'm not blowing Jordan at all. I'd be the first guy to tell him, "I'd love to see you play well but I'd love to see you guys lose."

DP: Give me the **worst physique in baseball.** A guy who does not belong in a baseball uniform.

MG: He's no longer on a team but I'd say John Kruk has to be there. Now admitting that I don't have a great body, if you want to say great players that don't have great bodies, Tony Gwynn would have to be up there.

DP: Let's settle this once and for all. **Are pitchers athletes?**

MG: Absolutely not. I say that emphatically. There is the occasional handful that are but for the most part they are not athletes.

DP: You don't seem obsessed with winning. It's a question that is not posed to you like Charles Barkley or Karl Malone, "When are you going to win your title?" Why is that?

MG: Because in basketball it is much easier for a great player to take over a game. And you cannot in baseball. For instance, if there's 15 seconds left in a tie game and you're the Chicago Bulls, you say get the ball to Michael and let him do something. In baseball, if you're in a tie game in the bottom of the ninth, you can't say, "OK, I want Mark Grace, Sammy Sosa and Henry Rodriguez to hit this inning."

DP: When it comes to baseball, who are the **three most knowledgeable celebrities you know?**

MG: Bill Murray. Can I say you?

DP: I don't want to be a celebrity.

MG: Then **Scott Simpson.** Here's a good name drop. **Bill Clinton.**

DP: Have you talked baseball with him?

MG: No, but I can say I did. I've seen him at Camden Yards. **Charles Barkley.** He's pretty knowledgeable.

DP: Name somebody you would want to face with the game on the line.

MG: Somebody coming off the DL. But there are two great pitchers that I have had success off of and that's Ramon Martinez and **John Smoltz.** Don't ask me why. Pedro Martinez, too. I've had good success against him over the years. It's weird. Three of the best in the game that I've done well off of.

DP: So you're a **better hitter against better pitchers?**

MG: I think if you go over the course of my career and you line up the best pitchers in the game my numbers against them will be as good or better than anyone else.

DP: Give me a pitcher you don't want to face.

MG: John Franco. He owns me. Greg McMichael owns me. Basically, anybody pitching in the Mets bullpen.

DP: Sid Fernandez owned you, didn't he?

MG: He broke two 19-game hitting streaks. The bastard.

DP: Sid Fernandez, speaking of bad bodies.

MG: He definitely had one.

DP: Give me the percentage of pitchers who cheat.

MG: I'd say probably **thirty percent.** You know scuffing, spitting, pine tar to make your forkball stick a little better.

DP: As a golfer and someone who deals with the etiquette of that game, does it bother you that they don't abide by the rules? And other players too, hitters, for that matter?

MG: I don't worry about it too much. **The more you gripe about it the more you sound like a whiner.** But I'll have balls checked if something comes up there that looks funny. If Orel Hershiser throws me something up there that acts funny, I'll check the ball. I've checked Mike Scott before. There are plenty of guys out there that cheat but it's not worth the hassle.

DP: Do you lose respect for pitchers on your own team who cheat?

MG: Absolutely not. I don't have a problem with pitchers who cheat at all, either on my team or against me. I've never done it but hitters use cork. Hitters cheat and pitchers cheat. You know the old adage,

"If you're not cheating, you're not trying."

I don't have a problem with it. Any way to get an edge. It's all about winning. If it helps you win and you don't get caught, it's not cheating.

DP: Percentage of players using steroid nowadays.

MG: Oh, mercy. Steroids? Or that creatine?

DP: Steroids, anything. Juice. Any performance-enhancing drug.

MG: I would say probably 50 to 60 percent are getting some kind of help.

DP: Has it ever entered your mind to cheat like that?

MG: No.

DP: Why? Afraid of needles?

MG: I would never take steroids because there are so many dangers to it. As far as creatine is concerned, there are still a lot of negative things coming back about it, that it can be bad for you. **Steroids are supposed to be bad for your sex life.**

DP: That's all you needed to hear!

MG: Can't have that!

DP: Name three players you would pay to see. Current or retired.

MG: **Babe Ruth,** certainly. **Roger Clemens.** And last but not least, **Mark McGwire.**

DP: Are you amazed at what he can do to a baseball?

MG: I'm amazed at the excitement he generates. We had a four-game series at Wrigley Field against the Cardinals and the Cub fans were giving him a standing ovation every time he came to the plate.

DP: And that's hard to do.

MG: Usually, when the great players come to town like Barry Bonds, Tony Gwynn, Gary Sheffield or Greg Maddux, they get booed. **They get booed beyond belief.** Mark McGwire gets cheered. And if he gets walked, it's "Boooooooo!" They come early to watch his batting practice. And you know how you bunt the first pitch of batting practice? They boo when he bunts it. Because they know that when he swings there's a chance he will hit it farther than we have ever seen a baseball be hit.

DP: How many **proms** were you invited to last year?

MG: (Laughs.) Four or five. I had to respectfully decline. I can't be hanging around with 17-year-old girls.

DP: What is it with athletes and all the scratching?

MG: Have you ever worn a cup? You realize that they are not very comfortable. It's not that we are scratching. **We are just adjusting because those damn things are very uncomfortable.** And they move around on you.

DP: Don't you think with all of our modern technology we could come up with a comfortable protective cup?

MG: I wish that we could. I would be glad to endorse it. I'd be like Jim Palmer in all the magazines, with my body and my cup.

DP: Are there any similarities between a great golf swing and a great batting stroke?

MG: A few. The hand-eye coordination. The club position versus bat position at impact are similar. The follow-through is also similar. The only thing is that **golfers get to play in complete peace and quiet.** I have to go out there and hit a fastball going ninety miles an hour while people are saying, "Grace, you suck! You asshole!"

DP: But they have to play their foul balls.

MG: And I get another pitch.

DP: How does the clubhouse music now compare to ten years ago?

MG: When I first got to the big leagues, guys like Rick Sutcliffe, Jody Davis and Goose Gossage were always playing country. When rap got popular, that took over. Now it's whatever the starting pitcher likes to listen to. Jeremi Gonzalez plays Latin music. When Mark Clark pitches we listen to country music. When Steve Trachsel pitches we listen to alternative rock music. When Kevin Tapani pitches, we listen to Howard Stern.

DP: What about Kerry Wood?

MG: He's 20 years old so we listen to lullabies.

DP: Last book you read?

MG: Clive Cussler's *Deep Six*. It's James Bond, superhero, action-adventure, underwater disaster kind of stuff.

DP: At least you didn't say *Penthouse Forum*. What are three things the Cubs need to be a World Series contender?

MG: We need production from other than the heart of the order, production from the top and bottom of the order. We need healthy and consistent starting pitching. **And we need the wind to blow out.**

My son is in love with Kobe

(T)alk about opposites: I knew we'd have nothing in common, but I just love the way he plays. He's the basketball version of Keyshawn Johnson in that he wants to win and he'll do whatever it takes to win.

At first Gary had the attitude, "You're not going to get inside my head." I had to build some trust before he was going to give me anything. I had to work a bit. Actually, I had to work pretty hard just to get him on the phone, but once we got going it was more than worth the effort.

I don't think he takes that sneer off when he leaves the basketball floor. That's him. A lot of guys are not like that. Gary's not acting out there. I noticed that he likes certain athletes who have the same style and approach. I think he appreciates them because he knows what it does for him.

The most lasting impression I have from my interview with Gary Payton is the sound of his voice. There was an edge to it, an edge that accompanies honesty. The tone of his voice said, "This is who I am. Deal with it." It gave me a real sense of what it must be like to play against him.

DP: What does the media not understand about being a professional athlete?

GP: The beat writers don't understand anything.
They come with you on the road, they look at basketball and then they try to evaluate you on your performance of things. And I don't think one of them played basketball in their life. So to me, the beat writers ain't nothing — a person that just wants to sell papers to me. That's it. And that's why I don't like dealing with them.

DP: What's the biggest thing that's misunderstood about you, though?

GP: Well, they don't understand me because when I'm playing basketball, I don't want to relate to them or I don't want to talk to them. And that's the problem. But when somebody gets to know me, they get to know me.

and it makes me upset.

DP: The average fan, what do you think they misunderstand about you?

GP: About me being a person. I'm not the person that they see on the basketball floor. To me, basketball is a business. It's something that I do. I can't take it as a fun thing right now. I gotta play basketball and when you're on the court, I'm nobody's friend and that's the attitude they see.

DP: How would you rate these haircuts? **Detlef Schrempf.**

GP: (Laughs.) He's got his own style. He got the little thing sticking up but you know, that's gutless. So I then got accustomed to it because I been around it for years. And it looks good on him but it wouldn't look good on me.

DP: Brian Grant.

GP: Brian got the little dreads. You know that's the new look. You know everybody's trying to get the corn rows and the dreads in their hair. And that ain't my style neither.

DP: Michael Jordan.

GP: That's me. Bald-headed, clean-cut, that's just me.

DP: Allen Iverson.

GP: Iverson's got the braids. Couldn't see them either on me. I mean that's their style. I don't think I could have that much and all the braids going different ways.

DP: # Give me the best Afro that ever played in the NBA.

GP: Artis Gilmore.

DP: I don't know what was in that thing. There could have been birds in there, I have no idea.

DP: Give me three guys that **you know you couldn't guard** in history.

GP: Oscar Robinson. He was a big guy, a big guard. And he had all the ability to post you up, rebound. He was real strong. And I think he would give me a lot of trouble.

DP: Okay.

GP: He would be like a forward but he would be playing guard. Like Magic Johnson. But I think he was a little bit quicker than Magic. **Magic is another one that I would have trouble guarding, too.**

DP: Anybody else?

GP: I would have to say Calvin Murphy. Because Calvin was one of them guys where when he was coming up they had the rein to hit you, bump you and he was so small that that's how he had to guard a guy.

DP: He's one of the toughest guys I've ever seen.

GP: And he would have probably beat me down and hurt me and all that stuff.

DP: What about Ice Gervin?

GP: Yeah. He was my idol coming up in basketball. I think you could have checked him on defense. Because **he didn't want to play defense.**

DP: Is there anybody you just say, I haven't figured him out yet?

GP: Rod Strickland. I think I haven't figured him out because I don't play him as much. He's a crafty guy — he gets to the basket so easy on me and I don't know why he does.

DP: What's the last CD you bought or listened to?

GP: **Snoop Doggy Dog, the rappers.**

DP: Well, now he's Snoop Dog. You don't have any MC Hammer in your collection.

GP: (Laughs.) No, he's gone out of the collection.

DP: Can Master P play hoops? Who plays like him in the NBA?

GP: I gotta think ... David Wingate.

DP: How would you describe David Wingate's game?

GP: David Wingate is one of them feisty little players. He's the type of guy that is gonna keep coming at you. And he's just a spirited guy and he loves the game.

DP: So that would be **Master P?**

GP: Yeah. And Master P is the kind of person who has talent but he doesn't have the talent that's gonna really get him there. But he's loved the game and he's gonna keep trying to play and he's gonna play hard.

DP: Being in Seattle, can you see a solution to keep A-Rod and Griffey in a Mariners uniform?

GP: I think owners are now thinking that well, I can't have two people on the team that I am paying 100 million apiece. It's gonna be worth more than my franchise. And that's the problem. There's no solution. But Griffey is the man in Seattle. A-Rod is an upcoming star in the league. But they probably will trade A-Rod because Ken Griffey is the future of the Seattle Mariners.

DP: If you could take something into the millennium, your family's going with you, but one thing that you say, "I gotta take this with me?"

GP: Probably **my gold medal from the Olympics.**
I would have to take that. That was a big part of my life, especially when I met Muhammad Ali. The Olympics was a great achievement for me.

DP: If you could trash talk anybody besides basketball guys, who would it be? Who would you just love to get into trash talking with?

GP: Muhammad Ali. I know he would come with some stuff.

DP: Do you have favorite athletes in other sports?

GP: **Barry Bonds.** He's so flashy, how he hits a homer and he drops the bat. Griffey. He and I are real tight from Seattle. Deion Sanders, because of all the flashy stuff he does. In basketball, **I love Antoine Walker from Boston. Because he does all that dancing stuff. I like that. I like that a lot.**

DP: What's your favorite movie?

GP: *Harlem Nights*. You got Richard Pryor, Eddie Murphy, **Redd Foxx,** all them guys. I looked at it the other day and it was so funny, **the funniest stuff I've ever seen in a movie.**

DP: If you were a cop, who would you arrest?

GP: I'd arrest all them referees. Every one of them.

DP: Would you arrest just the ones that cheated on their income tax or all the referees?

GP: I'd arrest every one of them.

DP: Your favorite children's book.

GP: *Green Eggs and Ham*. That was the silliest thing, the silliest book. "Green Eggs and Ham is why you am." All that crap. I was like, oh, my goodness.

DP: I think Dr. Seuss was smoking something.

DP: Doom or NBA Live?

GP: NBA Live.

DP: Are you real in NBA Live? I mean is that you? Have they captured your game?

GP: Not really. Not really. **You know most of them games, they got you in there dunking. That ain't me.**

DP: Who's the best player in the game?

GP: Right now, Scottie Pippen. As an all-around player, he is the best right now.

DP: Who's the worst dresser?

GP: It would have to be Karl Malone and John Stockton. They don't care what they wear. I'm serious, they don't. They wear the too-little jeans. The argyle shirts. The old style shirts with the crocodiles on them. Man.

DP: Or a flannel shirt.

GP: Yeah. If that's the way they want to do it . . .

DP: Well, I guess that — Hornacek is probably up there — maybe it's just the whole Utah team is the worst-dressed team.

DP: Did anyone ever really react to one of your taunts?

GP: Yeah, the guy on the New Jersey, the little forward on New Jersey. What's his name? The forward, he's a white guy.

DP: Keith Van Horn?

GP: Not Van Horn. He can play. This dude can't play. Can't play a lick. Say another name.

DP: Jamie Feick?

GP: Yeah, Jamie Feick. He said something to me. I said, **"Look here, man, you won't even be in the league next year."** And he's trying to say something to me. And then Scott Burrell came over and said I hurt his feelings.

DP: Do your kids root for other athletes besides you?

GP: My son is in love with Kobe Bryant. And it makes me upset. Every time. He wears his jersey around and runs around the house throwing the balls on the wall. Kobe Bryant and this and that. He loves Shaq, he loves Shaq to death too.

DP: Do you own a Shaq CD?

GP: I got every one of them. **I got every one of Shaq's CDs.**

DP: Give me an athlete who thinks he can rap.

GP: OP. Olden Polynice. He can't rap.

DP: You're going to hurt his feelings.

DP: Would you be able to describe George Karl's playing style?

GP: No. His style is ridiculous. We watched the tapes on him one time when he was here. I was like, **"I don't even know how you got in the league."**

DAN PATRICK   **DAVID CONE**

Chicks are not digging

(**I**) met David Cone in 1986 and did not really see the side of him that he shows in the interview. After that, I would see him occasionally and he'd come up and say, "I saw you on *SportsCenter* the other night. I love watching you guys." Even that fairly innocent remark meant something, because most athletes don't mention it even though you know they watch. Cone has never been the kind of guy who is above passing along a compliment.

That kind of security in who he is says a lot about David Cone. I think he appreciates what he has been able to accomplish and doesn't take it for granted. The professional respect he has always shown me allows any conversation I might have with him to be easy and natural. Of all the interviews I have done for the magazine, David Cone's was the most like a chat you'd have in a bar. Anything could come up and we'd just run with it. Inside stuff, silly stuff, serious stuff. Nothing off-limits.

When I called to do the "Outtakes," I knew I'd be talking to someone who knew my style and would be comfortable. Just how comfortable Mr. Cone was is evident in his very first answer.

DP: What is in your pockets right now?

DC: (Fumbling around.) Ummmm, nothing, unfortunately. Damn it! (Laughs.) Actually, I'm naked. (Laughs.) But I have my <u>**room key**</u> in the crack of my ass. (Laughs.) **Don't know if you can print that.**

DP: Oh, yeah, we can.

DC: OK.

DP: If I only had some video of this.

DP: What does it take to understand the media?

DC: You just can't take yourself too seriously.
But that's too serious of an answer.

ground balls.

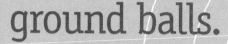

DP: Is there one thing about the media that bothers you?

DC: Yeah. When I first walk in the clubhouse, they can't even wait until I get dressed. They want to do interviews when you're half-naked. At least they could let you get dressed.

DP: You like the **Weather Channel?**

DC: Yes I do.

DP: Why?

DC: I like the music. Outstanding collaboration. (Laughs.)

DP: Doesn't Yanni do that soundtrack?

DC: Sometimes. I like Yanni. They mix it up though.

DP: A little Zamfir?

DC: Yeah. They get some Yanni going and some soft jazz.

DP: Greg Maddux says the sound of a home run is two cars crashing. How would you describe it?

DC: Like dropping a stack of dishes.

DP: Do you know the sound, though, as soon as you throw it?

DC: Yeah. You know the sound.

DP: Do you cringe?

DC: And you snap your head back. And maybe it's instinctual, for whatever reason, you know it's gone but you still snap your head back to watch it as if there is a chance it might stay in.

DP: **That's for effect, for TV.**

To make it seem like, "Oh, did he get all of that?"

DC: Mark Gubicza had it down. He'd just put his head down. He knew right away. The best I've ever seen. **He'd give up a home run and immediately his dauber was down.** He didn't even watch it.

DP: Have you ever had a great conversation on the mound? The catcher is trying to make you laugh. Or it has nothing to do with baseball.

DC: None that are G-rated.

DP: Oh, really?

DC: Girardi will come up with some things that will break the tension now and then.

DP: Give me an example. I'm not out there. And I can't just take your word, as a journalist.

DC: (Laughs.) One time Girardi came out to the mound and said, **"Look over at the dugout. Don Zimmer's going to moon you."** That's was the best line I ever heard. The bases were loaded and I couldn't throw a strike. (Laughs.)

DP: Do you remember who this was against?

DC: I think it was against Seattle. He knew I was flustered and he came out and dropped that line on me.

DP: Just out of curiosity, do you find yourself checking out Don Zimmer when he's naked?

DC: Well, I have noticed.

DP: **One day you will be that age and gravity will take over.**

DC: This is true. This is true.

DP: Give me your favorite Don Zimmer story or line.

DC: He had a great one the other day. This is fresh. We called a team meeting and he broke it up. He said, "You players want a team meeting, go rent a ballroom. Don't do it in here." (Laughs.)

DP: Is there any baseball advice that can be found in ***Chicken Soup for the Soul*?**

DC: Oh, yes. Without a doubt.

DP: Like?

DC: Well, **less is more.** Especially when you are pitching. A lot of times the problem is you are trying too hard. It's the Maddux theory. Take a little off and let them get themselves out. There are a lot of themes like that throughout that book. That's too serious. I can't think of anything funny for that one.

DP: Can you explain the whole next-batter-gets-hit-after-the-guy-homers thing? I still don't understand that.

DC: Never understood that. Don't understand that. And would never do it.

DP: **David Wells.** What is the one thing you miss most about him?

DC: Watching the sun come up with him. That's the thing... That's the worst and the best thing about him not being here.

DP: David does not get cheated in life, does he?

DC: No, he does not get cheated. He is living a full life.

DP: Do you have interest in seeing *The Phantom Menace?*

DC: Not desperately. But I probably will see it. It's not on the top of my list.

DP: Last movie you saw.

DC: *Saving Private Ryan.* But you don't really want to know the last movie I saw. It was one of those SpectraVision movies in my room. (Laughs.) **They claim the title won't appear on your bill.** So I can't remember what the name was.

DP: But you have worried about the title appearing on your bill?

DC: Well, not really. Once you get a bad rep, you can't shake it. So what's the matter?

DP: Do chicks dig the long ball?

DC: Most definitely. **Chicks do dig the long ball.**

DP: They don't dig striking out the guy who can hit the long ball?

DC: They are not digging ground balls. (Laughs.) **Managers dig ground balls.** Umpires dig ground balls and two-hour games. Chicks don't dig that.

DP: Mark Grace says that pitchers aren't athletes.

DC: Well, there is some truth to that. **But try getting drunk four nights a week and going out there to pitch nine innings. That's an athlete to me.** (Laughs.) Actually, I disagree with him.

DP: Give me a TV show that people would be surprised you watch.

DC: That would be (long pause) maybe **"Geraldo Rivera."** At night. (Laughs.)

DP: On what, CNBC?

DC: Especially during the whole Sexgate thing. Every night. Love that stuff.

DP: It was the same thing every night.

DC: But I could identify with it.

DP: You can? With Sexgate? (Laughs.) **Is there anything that goes on in the bullpen that we are not supposed to know about?**

DC: Now, now.

DP: If **Paul O'Neill** was your son and he threw one of his temper tantrums, what would you do as a parent?

DC: I'd slap him silly. (Laughs.) I would just slap him silly.

DP: Would you give him a time out?

DC: No time out. I don't believe in time out. My dad used to tell me to go get the stick. Choose. Your choice of weapons. Do you want the stick?

DP: I'm worried about Paul, though.

DC: The other night he had a tantrum and he came in and looked like he was in that movie *Scanners*. His head was going to explode. **He was beet red. And you thought his head was going to explode.**

DP: Doesn't he see himself on TV?

DC: I think he does. But right after the game he's fine. And he's the most mild-mannered, good-humored guy you could meet. Until the game starts. For three hours he's *Scanners*.

DP: And you stay away from him. Because it's guilt by association.

DC: You can't talk to him. You can't say anything to him when he is in that mode. You can talk to him later. We get all over him, joking all the time. He takes it very well.

DP: Do you have a secret desire to hug **George Steinbrenner?**

DC: No. **A handshake is fine.**

DP: Do you watch baseball? If you are not playing, do you care about baseball?

DC: Yes. Very much. I want to know what Maddux is doing to get those guys out. I want to know all the secrets, all the tricks.

DP: What can you pick up from watching a game?

DC: Style. Strategy. Patterns. **Watch Greg Maddux's pattern.** How he gets out tough lefties.

DP: Best pitcher of this era. Would he be among three guys you would say defined your era's starting pitching?

DC: Certainly. Clemens and Maddux have defined our era, I believe. And Randy Johnson is right behind them and still going.

DP: When was the last time somebody joked about hitting a home run off you?

DC: Actually, it happened the other night. I gave up one to Mike Stanley that was kind of **a Fenway Parker, barely got out.** He was joking with me that the wind blew it out. As former teammates, it's a little easier.

DP: But you weren't laughing?

DC: Sort of. It was the day after. I wasn't laughing that night. After a few beers, I was laughing. (Laughs.)

DP: Do you have an expression for a home run?

DC: I have a few, but...

DP: You can give them to me.

DC: **"Here's the pitch and ... you can grab your ankles!"** (Laughs.)

DP: Mike Piazza says you have to squat at parties to survey the scene.

DC: You have to squat? That's interesting.

DP: Any tips from a pitcher's standpoint? From your bachelor days.

DC: Bar tend. That's the place to be. **Behind the bar or near the women's rest room. Just hanging out by the wall.**

ISBN: 0-7868-8539-4

First Edition
10 9 8 7 6 5 4

PHOTO CREDITS:

Allsport: 73; Allsport/MSI 161 right; Al Bello 142 bottom; J. Daniel 37; Jon Ferrey 63; Stu Forster 49; Otto Greule 82; Tom Hauck 3, 8, 9, 152; Harry How 164 top; Robert LaBerge 47 top, 132 bottom; Andy Lyons 35 top, 135; Donald Miralle 44, 158; Adrian Morrell 138; D. Pensinger 134; Tom Pidgeon 52; Gary M. Prior cover (bottom), introduction, 116, 117; Eliot Schechter 80 top; Ezra Shaw 62, 99; Jamie Squire 27 top; Rick Stewart 146; David Taylor 26; Ian Tomlinson 68; Todd Warshaw 32

BBS Archive Photos: 72, 142 top

DeHoog/TDP: 30, 75, 78, 79, 81, 87, 92, 115, 136

Tom DiPace: 2, 5, 7 both, 10 top, 13, 28, 33, 45, 46 top, 50, 51, 54 top, 55, 56, 57, 58 both, 61, 65, 69, 70 bottom, 74, 85 top, 86, 91 both, 93, 95, 98, 100, 101 top, 103, 104, 105, 106, 109, 110, 111, 112, 118, 122 top, 123, 124, 127, 128, 129, 130, 140, 141, 145, 147, 149 both, 150, 153, 154, 156 top, 165, 166 bottom, 168, 169

Everett Collection: 36, 66 bottom, 76, 88, 97, 101 bottom, 114 bottom, 162 top

Everett/Robert Heplar: 107 top

Todd France: Dan Patrick photograph (cover and throughout), 48, 70 top

NBA Photos: Ray Amati 38; Andrew D. Bernstein 14, 42; Nathaniel S. Butler 39; Steve DiPaola 20; Garrett Ellwood 15 right; Barry Gossage 17; Glenn James 21 top; David Sherman 23; Noren Trotman 159; Rocky Widner 18 top

NBC/EC: 120

Photodisc: 4, 6, 10 bottom, 11, 12, 15 left, 18 bottom, 19, 21 bottom, 22, 25, 27 bottom, 29, 31, 34, 35 bottom, 40, 41, 43, 46 bottom, 47 bottom, 54 bottom, 60, 64, 66 top, 71 both, 77, 80 bottom, 83, 89 both, 90, 107 bottom, 108, 113 both, 114 top, 119, 121, 122 bottom, 125, 126, 132 middle, 137, 139, 148 both, 151, 156 bottom, 157, 161 left, 162 bottom, 164 bottom, 166 top, 167

plbsports.com: 85 bottom

Sean Roberts/Everett Collection: 132 top

UPI/Corbis-Bettmann: 24